QUICKHAND ⓉⓂ

QUICKHAND

JEREMY GROSSMAN, Ph.D.
Employee Development Systems

QUICKHAND Shorthand Learning Systems

JOHN WILEY & SONS
New York • Chichester • Brisbane • Toronto • Singapore

Editors: Judy Wilson and Irene Brownstone
Production Manager: Ken Burke
Editorial Supervisor: Winn Kalmon
Composition and Make-up: Frank Propellor
QUICKHAND written by: Alice Saitzeff Grossman

Library of Congress Cataloging in Publication Data

Grossman, Jeremy, 1942—
    Quickhand(TM) .

    (Wiley self-teaching guides)
    1. Shorthand—Quickhand. I. Title
Z56.G89   653'.2   75-42314
ISBN 0-471-32887-1

Printed in the United States of America

76 **77**   20 19 18 17 16

TO MY WIFE ALICE

AND TO OUR CHILDREN

JUDITH, DAVID AND JOSEPH

ACKNOWLEDGEMENTS

I am deeply indebted to thousands of students and hundreds of teachers who have provided me with validation data based upon their experiences with earlier QUICKHAND programs and have made suggestions to improve the program.

Among those who performed far above the call of duty in helping me improve the text are Mrs. Roberta Thompson of Casa Grande Union High School in Case Grande, Arizona, and Professor D. J. O'Dell of Central Arizona College in Coolidge, Arizona, and their many students.

I would especially like to thank Mrs. Marilyn Riley, who edited, proofread, and typed draft after draft of the text.

I would also like to thank my wife Alice and our children Judith, David, and Joseph, who have helped to provide the inspiration for the QUICKHAND project.

Of course, for any errors or shortcomings, I must accept responsibility myself.

Silver Spring, Maryland   J. G.
January, 1976

To the Reader

QUICKHAND is a new easy-to-learn approach to shorthand, for personal or professional use. It is a simple, practical, individualized alternative to traditional shorthand systems. With the self-teaching format of this book, you can learn QUICKHAND on your own, without formal classes. You learn QUICKHAND by actually writing it, right from the beginning. And you can learn at your own pace, with as much or as little practice as you like.

Every year nearly a million people begin a shorthand class. Only about 100,000 of them ever attain 80 words per minute. Shorthand, according to several studies, is the most failed subject in high school. That fact is even more astonishing since almost everybody can write 35 words a minute in English longhand. And just by getting used to writing fast and using a few standard abbreviations, most people can probably learn to write close to 60 words a minute with no training at all. Yet studies show that less than one student in five can write in shorthand at 60 words a minute after a year of class!

QUICKHAND aims to change that. Many people have difficulty with shorthand—not because they cannot learn, but because of the difficulty of traditional shorthand systems. But QUICKHAND is designed for easy learning and everyday use. In QUICKHAND you use letters of the alphabet (not a whole new set of symbols and variations, as in other systems). And QUICKHAND is based on a scientific study of actual language use. Thus, you learn special abbreviations only for words and word parts that are frequently used (not for words that are seldom used in practice). The words with special abbreviations in QUICKHAND are all among the fifty most-used English words. In addition, only the most frequently used words beginnings, word endings, and sounds within words are given special abbreviations. Therefore, with QUICKHAND you will learn all of the frequently used words, with a minimum of memorization. This QUICK-HAND program has been extensively tested and revised. As a result of these and other innovations, very few students fail or drop out of QUICK-HAND.

Now, if you would like to learn more about the history and development of QUICKHAND and other shorthand systems, and their comparative ease and difficulty, turn to the Appendix.

OBJECTIVES

Using this book, students will learn the QUICKHAND theory, including special abbreviations for the 35 most used words, and the most used word beginnings, word endings, and sounds which occur within words. They also will learn how to read material in QUICKHAND and to take short dictation exercises and write them back in English.

Students will attain a score of at least 90 on each of the chapter Self-Tests, and will complete the Final Test with no more than 20 errors.

At the end of their self-teaching program, students will be able to write QUICKHAND abbreviations for the 35 most used English words and write them back into English from their shorthand notes with at least 80 percent accuracy in writing shorthand outlines and 95 percent accuracy in writing back. They will also be able to write the correct shorthand for words containing the most used word beginnings, word endings, and sounds within words with the same accuracy standards as for the 35 most used words.

Students will also be able to take dictation for one minute at speeds of 50 words per minute and write it back from their own notes with an accuracy rating of 95 percent or higher.

If you are ready to teach yourself QUICKHAND, turn to "How to Use This Book." Good luck!

Contents

How to Use This Book

This book is designed so that you can learn QUICKHAND on your own, without ever attending a formal class. The material is presented in numbered sections called frames. Each frame will present some new material, and will give you a chance to practice and apply QUICKHAND as you learn. At each frame, answer the question, and then check your response with the correct answer given following the dashed line. To learn QUICKHAND most effectively, you must actually write it, so be sure you write your own answer before looking at the book's. As you read, be sure you cover up the book's answer (with an index card or a piece of paper) until you have written your own answer. If you make a mistake, correct it before you go on.

QUICKHAND is an alphabetical system of shorthand. Almost all material is written with letters of the alphabet. You do not have to learn a new set of symbols, because you already know the alphabet. In addition to using known symbols, the QUICKHAND system is simple and practical because it is based on studies of the English language as it is actually used in the office. Such studies show that only 10 words in the English language account for about a quarter of all words in office writing. Of every 100 words written, on the average, 25 of them will be one of these words: THE, OF, TO, AND, IN, YOU, A, FOR, WE, or YOUR. If you add 25 more words to this list, you will account for more than 40 percent of all words written in the office. In this book, you will have a special abbreviation for each of these 35 popular words. These abbreviations are called brief forms. When you learn to write these brief forms, you will know more than 40 percent of the QUICKHAND theory.

The rest of the theory is made up of easy abbreviations for word beginnings (such as DIS in DISCUSS and MIS in MISTAKE), word endings (such as ING in THINKING and TION in LOTION), and sounds that occur frequently within words (such as NK in BANKER and RD in CARDIAC). This material is not difficult, and you will begin to grasp it quickly with this book's self-teaching approach. Once you learn this material, you know QUICKHAND.

QUICKHAND will let you cut down on the physical act of writing by more than three-fifths. For every five letters of the alphabet you write in English, you will write less than two letters in QUICKHAND. And you will have learned special symbols only for the most used parts of the language.

When you finish this book, you will probably be writing between 50 and 60 words per minute. If you wish to build higher speeds (80 words per minute is the usual job level requirement) you will have to practice dictation and transcription. If you already write 35 words per minute in longhand, which is about average, you should be able to write about 90 words per minute in QUICKHAND. If you can force your longhand speed to 40 words per minute, you should be able to write QUICKHAND at more than 100 words per minute. Both of these figures are above the standard job requirements.

This book has been carefully designed so that you learn QUICKHAND step-by-step as you work through the program. If you follow the instructions given here, you should learn all you need to know about QUICKHAND by the time you finish the book. Never try to memorize lists of words. That will only slow you down. It would be as ridiculous to try to memorize a list of phone numbers. You will learn your words the same way you learn phone numbers—by using them over and over again.

At the end of each chapter is a Self-Test, to help you evaluate your progress with QUICKHAND. Correct answers are given at the end of the test. If you answer all Self-Test questions correctly, you are ready to go on to the next chapter. Be sure to correct mistakes before you proceed. At the back of the book, Supplementary Exercises are provided for Chapters 2 through 5, and you will find a comprehensive Final Test and a Glossary of brief forms, word endings, word beginnings, and sounds within words that make up the QUICKHAND system. A discussion of the history and development of QUICKHAND and other shorthand systems is also included.

Now turn to Chapter 1 and begin to teach yourself QUICKHAND.

QUICKHAND ™

Chapter One

1. The first rule of QUICKHAND, and the most important one, is to write words the way they sound. All QUICKHAND words are written as they sound. You can probably read the word below even though you may not have studied QUICKHAND until just now.

    Write in the blank provided what you think the following word is. $\mathcal{u}$

    _____

    - - - - - - - - - - - - - - - -

    The word you were looking at is YOU.

2. The word in frame 1 is an example of writing the way words sound. You ignore the way the word is spelled and write it the way it sounds.

    Can you read this word? $\mathcal{c}$ _____

    - - - - - - - - - - - - - - - -

    You just saw the word SEE or SEA.

3. In the above frame, how do you know which you mean? If you say

    LET'S $\mathcal{c}$, are you writing SEE or SEA?   _____

    - - - - - - - - - - - - - - - -

    You are writing SEE, of course. Whenever a word can have more than one meaning, you can always tell what you mean by the way it is used.

4. Are you grasping the principle of programmed instruction? You see that you never move ahead until you are given the answers to material which came earlier. Hopefully, you understand the answers thoroughly. If the material is simple, you may skip over it in a few seconds. If it is difficult, you may spend as much time as necessary on it.

What is this word? *dg* _____

- - - - - - - - - - - - - -

DOG, DIG, or DUG

5.   What is the word in this sentence? OUR *dg*   HAD A LITTER OF PUPPIES. _____

- - - - - - - - - - - - - - -

Of course, the correct word is DOG. The other choices would be ridiculous.

6.   When a word in QUICKHAND can be more than one word in longhand, one possibility will always make sense and the others will not when read in the sentence.
    Now, try this word. *kt* _____

- - - - - - - - - - - - - - -

CAT, KIT, or CUT

7.   Now try this word. *btr* _____

- - - - - - - - - - - - - - -

BATTER, BETTER, BITTER, or BUTTER

8.   What is *btr* in this sentence? THERE ARE THREE BALLS AND A STRIKE ON THE *btr* . _____

- - - - - - - - - - - - - - -

BATTER, of course

9.   Read the same QUICKHAND in the following sentences.
    (a) I HOPE TO FEEL *btr*   AFTER I SEE THE DOCTOR. _____
    (b) HE IS *btr*   THAT HE DID NOT GET THE PROMOTION.

    _____

    (c) PLEASE PASS THE BREAD AND *btr* . _____

- - - - - - - - - - - - - - -

(a) BETTER; (b) BITTER; (c) BUTTER   (In each case, any other word would be ridiculous.)

10. In English, we dot the I and the J. In QUICKHAND, we do not. The I and J are written ι, $\jmath$.

Now, write the I and J. _____

- - - - - - - - - - - - - - - -

11. Read these letters. ι, $\jmath$ _____
- - - - - - - - - - - - - - - -

I, J

12. In English, we cross the T. In QUICKHAND, we do not. The T is written ι .

Try writing the T. _____

- - - - - - - - - - - - - - - -

13. Now, read these letters. ι, $\jmath$, ι _____
- - - - - - - - - - - - - - - -

I, J, T

14. You will cross the X in QUICKHAND, because if you do not, you might have a hard time reading it back.

When you write E in QUICKHAND, be sure to put a large loop in it. Also, be careful not to put any loop in the I. E and I should be written as follows: ℓ , ι .

Also, be careful to put a large loop in your L and not to put any loop in your T, in order to avoid confusion when reading back. You should write L and T like this: ℓ , ι .

(a) Now, write I, J, and T. _____

(b) Write E and L. _____

- - - - - - - - - - - - - - - -

(a) ι $\jmath$ ι ; (b) ℓ ℓ

Could you tell the difference between your I and E and between your L and your T?

15. All other letters are written just the same in QUICKHAND as they are in regular English.

Now, let's take a look at some more writing as words sound.

What do you think this word is? *ltr* (Notice that the T is not crossed.) _____

- - - - - - - - - - - - - - -

That word is LETTER.

16. Read this word. *bk* _____

- - - - - - - - - - - - - - -

BACK or BOOK

17. What is this word? *abv* _____

- - - - - - - - - - - - - - -

ABOVE

18. What is this word? *mtr* _____

- - - - - - - - - - - - - - -

MATTER or METER

19. What is this word? *pln* _____

- - - - - - - - - - - - - - -

PLAN

20. Now, let's look at another principle of writing as words sound.

How would the word CAT begin if it were spelled the way it sounds?

_____

- - - - - - - - - - - - - - -

CAT would start with a *k* .

21. How would CAR begin? _____ How would the word CAN begin? _____

- - - - - - - - - - - - - - -

Both CAR and CAN begin with the sound of *k* .

22. You see that many words that are spelled with a C sound as if they are spelled with a K. In QUICKHAND, you will write them as they sound, with a K.
    Read these words. *km, kn, krl* _____

- - - - - - - - - - - - - - -

COME or CAME, CAN, CART

23. There are also C words that sound differently. How would you start the word CERTAIN if you were to spell it as it sounds?

_____

- - - - - - - - - - - - - - -

CERTAIN would start with the *s* .

24. How would the word CERTIFICATE start if it were spelled as it sounds? _____

- - - - - - - - - - - - - - -

CERTIFICATE would also start with the *s* .

25. You have noticed that most C words in English sound as if they begin with a K or an S. As you write words the way they sound, you write these words with a *k* or *s* .
    Now, read these words. *klm, kmpln, snlr, slr*

_____

- - - - - - - - - - - - - - -

CLAIM or CLIMB, COMPLAIN, CENTER, CELLAR or SELLER

26. Now, write these words.

    (a) CLEAN _____   (c) CERTAIN _____

    (b) CLEAR _____

- - - - - - - - - - - - - - -

(a) *kln*   ; (b) *klr*   ; (c) *srln*

27. Remember that <u>vowels</u> are the letters A, E, I, O, and U. Most of the time these letters can be eliminated in writing QUICKHAND, as they are not often major sounds.

Try reading the words below. Notice the vowels are eliminated in all of them.

(a) *c* _____

(b) *dg* _____

(c) *kl* _____

(d) *btr* _____

- - - - - - - - - - - - - - -

(a) SEE or SEA; (b) DOG, DIG, or DUG; (c) CAT, COT, CUT, or KIT; (d) BETTER, BATTER, BITTER, or BUTTER.

28. There are many sounds which you hardly hear in the English language. In the word EXCEPT, there are several letters which are almost silent. What are these letters? _____

- - - - - - - - - - - - - - -

In EXCEPT, the E's are vowels which are hardly heard and the T is almost silent.

29. The C in EXCEPT sounds like an S. How would you write EXCEPT in QUICKHAND? _____

- - - - - - - - - - - - - - -

EXCEPT is written *xsp* .

30. What else could the word *xsp* stand for? _____

- - - - - - - - - - - - - - -

It could also be ACCEPT

31. Look at the word LIFT. What letters are unnecessary in writing LIFT? _____

- - - - - - - - - - - - - - -

The T at the end of LIFT is not needed. And, of course, you may eliminate the vowel I.

32. How would you write LIFT in QUICKHAND? _____

- - - - - - - - - - - - - - -

lf

33. What other words could *ℓf* represent? _____

- - - - - - - - - - - - - - -

It could also be LEFT, LOFT, or LIFE. (As we have already learned, you can tell which word it represents by its use in the sentence.)

34. Which letters can be eliminated in the word WORLD?

_____

- - - - - - - - - - - - - - -

The D at the end of WORLD can be eliminated. The vowel O is also unnecessary in QUICKHAND.

35. How would you write WORLD in QUICKHAND? _____

- - - - - - - - - - - - - - -

wrl

36. What else could *wrl* stand for? _____

- - - - - - - - - - - - - - -

wrl could also be WHIRL

37. What letters are not necessary in the word NEXT when you write in QUICKHAND? _____

- - - - - - - - - - - - - - -

In NEXT, you may leave out the T at the end and the vowel E.

38. How would you write NEXT in QUICKHAND? _____

- - - - - - - - - - - - - - -

nx

39. What else could *nx* stand for? _____

- - - - - - - - - - - - - - -

nx could be NIX, NICKS, or KNOCKS.

40. You have seen that you rarely need to write vowels. Also, in the words EXCEPT, LIFT, WORLD, and NEXT, the last letters are almost silent. In combinations such as PT, FT, LD, and XT, the last letter is usually not needed when you write in QUICKHAND.

 See if you can read the following words written in QUICKHAND.

 (a) *lx* _____

 (b) *kl* _____

 (c) *nf* _____

- - - - - - - - - - - - - - -

(a) TEXT, TAX, TACKS, or TICKS; (b) CALL, KILL, or COLD;
(c) RAFT or RIFT

41. Again, don't confuse yourself by trying to learn rules. By seeing, reading, and eventually writing many examples, you will learn to apply the rules.

 You have already made substantial progress in reading QUICK-HAND. See if you can read some more words.

 Start with *u* . _____

- - - - - - - - - - - - - -

That is YOU.

42. Now, what is *c* ? _____

- - - - - - - - - - - - - - -

SEE or SEA

43. What is *dg* ? _____

- - - - - - - - - - - - - - -

DOG, DIG, or DUG

44. What is *kl* ? _____

- - - - - - - - - - - - - - -

CAT, KIT, COT, or CUT

45. What is this word? *blr* _____

- - - - - - - - - - - - - -

 BATTER, BETTER, BITTER, or BUTTER

46. What is *ll* ? _____

- - - - - - - - - - - - - -

TELL, TALL, or TALE

47. What is *ll* ? _____

- - - - - - - - - - - - - -

LET, LOT, LIT, or LATE

48. What is *slr* ? _____

- - - - - - - - - - - - -

CELLAR or SELLER

49. What is this word? *kr* _____

- - - - - - - - - - - - - -

CAR

50. What is *smnl* ? _____

- - - - - - - - - - - - - -

CEMENT

51. What is *xsp* ? _____

- - - - - - - - - - - - - -

EXCEPT or ACCEPT

52. What is *lf* ? _____

- - - - - - - - - - - - - -

LEFT, LIFT, LOFT, or LIFE

53. What is *wrl* ? _____

- - - - - - - - - - - - - -

WORLD or WHIRL

54. What is *kl* ? _____

- - - - - - - - - - - - - -

CALL, KILL, or COLD

55. What is *ny* ?   _____

- - - - - - - - - - - - - - -

NEXT, NIX, NICKS, or KNOCKS

56. What is   *pce* ?   _____

- - - - - - - - - - - - - -

PERCEIVE

57. Now, you try your hand. In the next few frames, write the given
    words in QUICKHAND.

    (a) YOU _____   (c) DOG _____

    (b) SEE _____   (d) CAT _____

- - - - - - - - - - - - - -

    (a) *u*   ; (b) *c*   ; (c) *dg* ; (d) *kl*

58. Remember that the T is not crossed. Write the following words.

    (a) BATTER _____

    (b) TELL _____

    (c) LET _____

- - - - - - - - - - - - - -

    (a) *blr*   ; (b) *ll*   ; (c) *ll*

59. Now, let's practice writing words with C spellings.

    (a) CIGAR _____

    (b) CAR _____

    (c) CEMENT _____

- - - - - - - - - - - - - - -

    (a) *sgr*   ; (b) *kr*   ; (c) *smnl*   (Again, the T is not
    crossed.)

60. Try the following words.

(a) EXCEPT _____   (d) COLD _____

(b) LIFT _____   (e) NEXT _____

(c) WORLD _____   (f) RAFT _____

- - - - - - - - - - - - - - - -

(a) *xsp* ; (b) *lf* ; (c) *wrl* ; (d) *kl* ;

(e) *nx* ; (f) *rf*

61. Now, you are ready to begin reading complete sentences. Try for a
    minute or two to read each sentence and write down what you think
    the QUICKHAND sentence is. When you think you have it, or when
    you have done as well as you can, check the answer.

    Start by reading this sentence. *i c u,* _____

- - - - - - - - - - - - - - - -

    I SEE YOU.

62. Now, read this. *i wl c u n 1 r.*

    _____

- - - - - - - - - - - - - - - -

    I WILL SEE YOU IN ONE HOUR.

63. Now, read this. *i wl c u n 1 r n r kr.*

    _____

- - - - - - - - - - - - - - - -

    I WILL SEE YOU IN ONE HOUR IN OUR CAR.

64. Now, read this. *i wl xpk 2 c u at 10.*

    _____

- - - - - - - - - - - - - - - -

    I WILL EXPECT TO SEE YOU AT TEN.

65. Now, try to write these sentences in QUICKHAND. Do the best you
    can, but do not be upset if your QUICKHAND is not exactly as that in
    the book.

First, write I SEE YOU. _____

- - - - - - - - - - - - - -

ι c u .

66. Now, write I WILL SEE YOU IN ONE HOUR.

_____

- - - - - - - - - - - - - -

ι wl c u m l r.

67. Now, write I WILL SEE YOU IN ONE HOUR IN OUR CAR.

_____

- - - - - - - - - - - - - -

ι wl c u m l r m r kr.

68. Now, write I WILL EXPECT TO SEE YOU AT TEN.

_____

- - - - - - - - - - - - - -

ι wl xpk 2 c u at 10.

You have now completed Chapter 1. The most important concept
in this lesson is to write words as they sound. If you wish to review
reading and writing, you may turn back to frame 61. (Reading is much
more important at this point in the course than writing.)

SELF-TEST

A. Write the following words in QUICKHAND.

(1) LIFE _____ (3) CAME _____

(2) SEE _____ (4) NEXT _____

B. Transcribe the following words into English.

(1) *dg* _____ (3) *slsfe* _____
(2) *kl* _____ (4) *u* _____

C. Write the following sentences in QUICKHAND.

(1)   I WANT TO DRIVE YOUR CAR SOON.

---

(2)   YOU ARE TO SEE HER IN ONE DAY.

D.   Transcribe the following sentences.

(1)   *ι ℓm 2 c u.*

---

(2)   *ι wℓ c u n 1 r.*

Answers

A.   (1) *ℓf* ;   (2) *c*   ;   (3) *ℓm* ;   (4) *ny*

B.   (1) DOG;   (2) CAT, CUT, KIT, COT;   (3) SATISFY;   (4) YOU

C.   (1) *ι wnl 2 drv u kr sn.*

    (2) *u r 2 c hr n 1 da.*

D.   (1) I CAME TO SEE YOU.

    (2) I WILL SEE YOU IN ONE HOUR.

Chapter Two

1. In this chapter you will learn abbreviated QUICKHAND notations for some of the most frequently used word beginnings and word endings, as well as for the ten most popular words used in office correspondence.

   What is the word beginning in the following words? MISDIAL, MISSPELL, MISTAKE _____

   \- - - - - - - - - - - - - -

   MIS

2. What is the word beginning in these words? COMPEL, COMPROMISE, COMMAND _____

   \- - - - - - - - - - - - - -

   COM

3. What is the beginning in DISDAIN, DISJOINT, DISCUSS, DISPLEASE?

   _____

   \- - - - - - - - - - - - - -

   DIS

4. What is the beginning in CONCEAL, CONTRACT, CONTROL?

   _____

   \- - - - - - - - - - - - - -

   CON

5.   What is the beginning in OVERPASS, OVERTAKE, OVERHAND?

_____

- - - - - - - - - - - - - - - -

OVER

6.   What is the word beginning in UNDERHAND, UNDERWORLD,

UNDERDOG?   _____

- - - - - - - - - - - - - - - -

UNDER

7.   Look at the words MISTAKE and MISDIAL written in QUICKHAND
below, to see if you can tell how MIS is written. Write how MIS
should appear.

mlk , *mdl*   _____

- - - - - - - - - - - - - - - -

MIS is written with *m* .

8.   See if you can read the words in this and the following frames.

mkl   _____

- - - - - - - - - - - - - - - -

MISCALL

9.   What is this word? *mdl*   _____

- - - - - - - - - - - - - - - -

MISDIAL or MISDEAL

10. What is this word? *mdrk*   _____

- - - - - - - - - - - - - - - -

MISDIRECT. Notice DIRECT. The CT sounds like a K so it is
written with a *k* .

11. What is this word? *mlrs*   _____

- - - - - - - - - - - - - - - -

MISTRESS or MATTRESS

12. You would know which word is meant of the two in frame 11 by the way it is used in the sentence. Read the words in the two places in this sentence:

THE ____*mlrs*____ IS LYING ON THE ____*mlrs*____ .

- - - - - - - - - - - - - - -

Of course, there the sentence would be THE MISTRESS IS LYING ON THE MATTRESS. (It could not be "The mattress is lying on the mistress.")

13. You have seen that the MIS is written with an *m* . Can you guess how to write DIS?
     The words DISDAIN and DISPLEASE are written below.

ddn   *dplz*

Can you tell how DIS is written?   _____

- - - - - - - - - - - - - - -

The word beginning DIS is written *d* .

14. Now read the word below and the words in the following frames.

dlrb   _____

- - - - - - - - - - - - - - -

DISTURB

15. What is this word? *dkmfrl*   _____

- - - - - - - - - - - - - - -

DISCOMFORT

16. What is this word? *dks*   _____

- - - - - - - - - - - - - - -

DISCUSS

17. What is this word? *dkrb*   _____

- - - - - - - - - - - - - - -

DESCRIBE

18. Don't worry when DIS is spelled DES. In QUICKHAND, you are concerned only with the way words sound.

    Now, you have learned that MIS is written with an *m* and DIS is written with a *d* . Can you guess how COM at the beginning of a word is written? The words COMPEL and COMMAND are written below.

    kpl   *kmnd*

    Can you tell how COM is written? _____

    - - - - - - - - - - - - - - -

    COM is written with a *k* .

19. Can you read the word below and the words in the following frames?

    kprs   _____

    - - - - - - - - - - - - - - -

    COMPRESS

20. What is *kpr* ? _____

    - - - - - - - - - - - - - - -

    COMPARE

21. What is this? *kfrt*   _____

    - - - - - - - - - - - - - - -

    COMFORT

22. The COM is written with a *k* . How do you think the CON is written? The words CONCEAL, CONTRACT, and CONTROL are written below.

    ksl   *klrk*   *klrl*

    Can you tell how CON is written? _____

    - - - - - - - - - - - - - - -

    CON is also written with a *k* .

23. Now, read the word below and the words in the following frames.

    kvk   _____

    - - - - - - - - - - - - - - -

CONVICT (Again, notice that the CT at the end of the word sounds like a K, so it is written with a *k* .)

24. What is this word? *kvnk* _____

- - - - - - - - - - - - - -

CONVENT

25. What is this word? *kvrk* _____

- - - - - - - - - - - - - -

CONVERT

26. The words OVERPASS and OVERHAND are written below.

ops   *ohnd*   Can you tell how OVER is written? _____

- - - - - - - - - - - - - -

OVER is written with an *o* .

27. Now, read the QUICKHAND below and in the following frames.

oal _____

- - - - - - - - - - - - - -

OVERALL

28. What is this word? *olk* _____

- - - - - - - - - - - - - -

OVERTAKE

29. Now, read this. *oksl* _____

- - - - - - - - - - - - - -

OVERCAST

30. You have seen that OVER is written with an *o* . How do you think UNDER is written? The words UNDERHAND and UNDERPASS are written below.

uhnd   *ups*

Can you tell how UNDER is written? _____

- - - - - - - - - - - - - - -

UNDER is written with a *u* .

31. What is this word? *uwrl* _____

- - - - - - - - - - - - - - -

UNDERWORLD

32. Now, read this. *udg* _____

- - - - - - - - - - - - - - -

UNDERDOG

33. Now, read this word. *ulk* _____

- - - - - - - - - - - - - - -

UNDERTAKE or UNDERTOOK

34. You have now had one-third of the word beginnings you will study.
    But, these are the one-third that are most often used. You should
    have noticed that all the word beginnings are abbreviated with one
    letter. Shortened word beginnings and word endings are a major
    reason you can write several times faster in QUICKHAND than you
    can in English.
        Before you go on, read some more words written in QUICKHAND.

    What is this word? *dlns* _____

- - - - - - - - - - - - - - -

    DISTANCE

35. What is this word? *kmnd* _____

- - - - - - - - - - - - - - -

    COMMAND

36. What is this word? *klrl* _____

- - - - - - - - - - - - - - -

    CONTROL

37. What is this word? *olnd* _____

- - - - - - - - - - - - - -

OVERLAND

38. What is this word? *ukvr* _____

- - - - - - - - - - - - -

UNDERCOVER

39. What is the word ending in these words? EATING, DRINKING, TALKING _____

- - - - - - - - - - - - - -

ING

40. What is the ending in BASEMENT, ABATEMENT, and MOVEMENT?

_____

- - - - - - - - - - - - - -

The ending in these words is MENT

41. What is the ending in these words? TABLE, CAPABLE, MOVABLE

_____

- - - - - - - - - - - - - -

The word ending is BLE.

42. What is the ending in these words?

(a) ACTION, ATTENTION, MOTION _____

(b) OFFICIAL, INITIAL, PARTIAL _____

- - - - - - - - - - - - - -

(a) The ending is TION; (b) The ending is SHUL. (Sometimes SHUL is spelled CIAL or TIAL.)

43. What is the ending in these words? SPACIOUS, GRACIOUS, NOXIOUS _____

- - - - - - - - - - - - - -

SHUS (It is sometimes spelled TIOUS as in CAUTIOUS.)

44. Let's turn now to the ING. Can you tell how it is written from the words COMING, EATING, and MISSING below?

k.   *el.*   *m.*   _____

- - - - - - - - - - - - - - - -

You are right if you said that ING is written with a period, like this: . . As it is the most used word ending in English, it is the shortest and quickest to write.

45. Now, let's identify some ING words. What is this word? *rl.*

_____

- - - - - - - - - - - - - - - -

WRITING

46. What is *llk.* ? _____

- - - - - - - - - - - - - -

TALKING

47. What is *wlk.* ? _____

- - - - - - - - - - - - - -

WALKING

48. Now, can you tell how the MENT is written from the words AMAZE-MENT, MOVEMENT, and EXCITEMENT?

amzm   *mvm*   *xslm*   _____

- - - - - - - - - - - - - -

The MENT is written with *m* .

49. What is this word? *lrlm*   _____

- - - - - - - - - - - - - -

TREATMENT

50. What is this word? *mvm*   _____

- - - - - - - - - - - - - -

MOVEMENT

51. What is this word? *pam* _____

- - - - - - - - - - - - - -

PAYMENT

52. Can you see from the words ACTIVE, MOTIVE, and NATIVE below how the TIVE is written?

    akv   mv   nv _____

- - - - - - - - - - - - - -

TIVE is written with a *v* .

53. What is this word? *kprv* _____

- - - - - - - - - - - - - -

COMPARATIVE (Notice that this word has both a word beginning and a word ending.)

54. What is this word? *rlv* _____

- - - - - - - - - - - - - -

RELATIVE

55. What is this word? *slkv* _____

- - - - - - - - - - - - - -

SELECTIVE

56. Can you tell from the words TABLE, CAPABLE, and MOVABLE how the BLE is written?

    lb   kpb   mvb _____

- - - - - - - - - - - - - -

BLE is written with a *b* .

57. What is this word? *kb* _____

- - - - - - - - - - - - - -

CABLE

58. What is *mub* ? _____

- - - - - - - - - - - - - -

MOVABLE

59. What is *lb* ? _____

- - - - - - - - - - - - - -

TABLE

60. What is *lb* ? _____

- - - - - - - - - - - - - -

LABEL

61. The words ATTENTION, CONFUSION, and DEMONSTRATION are
written below. Can you tell how the SHUN sound is written? (Again,
don't be concerned with the spelling of the sound, just the pronunciation.)

alny kfuy dmnslry _____

- - - - - - - - - - - - - -

The SHUN sound is written with a *j* . Remember, the *j*   is
not dotted.

62. What is this word? *my* _____

- - - - - - - - - - - - - -

That word is MOTION.

63. What is *ly* ? _____

- - - - - - - - - - - - - -

LOTION

64. What is *ny* ? _____

- - - - - - - - - - - - - -

NATION or NOTION

65. Look at the words PARTIAL and SPECIAL and see if you can tell how the SHUL sound is written.

pry *spy* _____

- - - - - - - - - - - - - -

The SHUL sound is written with *y* .

66. What is this word? *pry* _____

- - - - - - - - - - - - -

PARTIAL

67. What is this word? *ofy* _____

- - - - - - - - - - - - -

OFFICIAL

68. What is this word? *mry* _____

- - - - - - - - - - - - -

MARTIAL

69. Can you tell from the words SPACIOUS and GRACIOUS how the SHUS sound is written?

spy *gry* _____

- - - - - - - - - - - - - -

The SHUS is also written with *y* . You can tell whether you want SHUL or SHUS by the way the word appears in the sentence.

70. What is this word? *jdy* _____

- - - - - - - - - - - - -

JUDICIOUS

71. What is this word? *nvx* _____

- - - - - - - - - - - - -

VIVACIOUS

72. You have now had about half of the word endings that you will study. Let's review them by reading the words in this and the following frames.

What is this word? *br.* _____

- - - - - - - - - - - - - - -

BRING

73. What is this word? *n.* _____

- - - - - - - - - - - - - - -

RING

74. What is this word? *mvm* _____

- - - - - - - - - - - - - - -

MOVEMENT

75. What is this word? *dlkv* _____

- - - - - - - - - - - - - - -

DETECTIVE

76. What is this word? *lvb* _____

- - - - - - - - - - - - - - -

LIVABLE or LOVABLE

77. Now, what is this word? *alny* _____

- - - - - - - - - - - - - - -

ATTENTION

78. What is this word? *prx* _____

- - - - - - - - - - - - - - -

PARTIAL

79. Now, what is this word? *grx* _____

- - - - - - - - - - - - - - -

GRACIOUS

80. Let's begin some QUICKHAND Shorthand writing. Remember the
    MIS. Write MISTAKE. _____

    - - - - - - - - - - - - - -

    mlk

81. Now, try a word with DIS. Write DISBAND. _____

    - - - - - - - - - - - - - -

    dbnd

82. Now, write a COM word: COMPARE. _____

    - - - - - - - - - - - - - -

    kpr

83. Now, write a CON word: CONVICT. _____

    - - - - - - - - - - - - - -

    kvk

84. Now, write a word with OVER: OVERPASS. _____

    - - - - - - - - - - - - - -

    ops

85. Now, write an UNDER word: UNDERPASS. _____

    - - - - - - - - - - - - - -

    ups

86. Now, let's turn to word endings. Write the word SING, with the
    ending ING. _____

    - - - - - - - - - - - - - -

    s .

87. Now, write MOVEMENT, with the ending MENT. _____

    - - - - - - - - - - - - - -

    mvm

88. Now, write the word MOTIVE, with the ending TIVE. _____

- - - - - - - - - - - - - - -

mv

89. Now, write a word ending in BLE: CABLE. _____

- - - - - - - - - - - - - - -

kb

90. Now, write a word with the SHUN ending: EDITION. _____

- - - - - - - - - - - - - - -

edy

91. Now, write a SHUL word: OFFICIAL. _____

- - - - - - - - - - - - - - -

ofx

92. Now, write a SHUS word: SPACIOUS. _____

- - - - - - - - - - - - - - -

spx

If you want to review some more, turn back to frame 80. Otherwise, move ahead to the next frame.

93. When you write in QUICKHAND, you will use regular punctuation.

Indicate a new paragraph by making two lines like this: **//** . Then continue writing.

Use regular capitalization. Do not capitalize the first word of a sentence, since it is not necessary when reading back the material.

Ten English words—THE, OF, TO, AND, IN, YOU, A, FOR, WE, and YOUR—make up about one-quarter of all words that are written in the office. Each of these ten words is abbreviated with one letter or symbol. These abbreviations are called brief forms. Do not try to memorize these words. You will learn them by using them over and over in sentences. The next frames give you these words with an opportunity to discover for yourself how most of them are written.

The word THE is used in English more often than any other word. Because it is used frequently, it can be written very quickly with

just a dash, like this: ▬ .

The other brief forms in this lesson will be written either with one letter or with a standard abbreviation. The second most used word in English is OF. How would you spell OF if you spelled it the way it sounds? Spell it as it sounds when you are not too careful with your pronunciation. _____

- - - - - - - - - - - - - -

You would spell OF: UV.

94. Write OF with its dominant sound. _____

- - - - - - - - - - - - - -

OF is written: $\mathcal{N}$.

95. The third most used word is TO. You can write it with the number 2. How would you write it? _____

- - - - - - - - - - - - - -

$\mathcal{2}$

96. The next word, the fourth most popular, is AND. AND has a standard abbreviation. It is written with the ampersand: ϕ .

- - - - - - - - - - - - - -

97. The remaining words in the ten most popular are all written with the first dominant sound.
   How do you think you would write IN, the fifth most popular word?

_____

- - - - - - - - - - - - - -

IN is written $\mathcal{n}$.

98. How about word number six, YOU? _____

- - - - - - - - - - - - - -

The word YOU is written as it sounds: μ .

99. The next word, number seven, is A. That should be easy for you.

_____

- - - - - - - - - - - - - -

A is written: *a* .

100. The next word, number eight, is WE. How do you think you write

WE?   _____

- - - - - - - - - - - - - -

w

101. Word number nine is FOR. You can get a hint from the way you
write TO on how to write FOR. It can also be written with the first

dominant sound. How do you write FOR?   _____

- - - - - - - - - - - - - -

You write FOR: *4* . (Or you may write it with *f* .)

102. The tenth most used word is YOUR. Write it with the first dominant

sound.   _____

- - - - - - - - - - - - - -

Write YOUR with a *u* . It is written the same way as YOU.
You can tell which word you want, YOU or YOUR, by the way it is
used in the sentence.

103. Each of the ten brief forms presented in this lesson comes up frequently in your writing and each can be written quickly. With a little practice, these ten brief forms should become very easy to remember. Let's begin our practice now.

   Do you recognize this word? *—*   _____

- - - - - - - - - - - - - -

THE

104. What is this word? *v*   _____

- - - - - - - - - - - - - -

OF

105. What is this? *2*   _____

- - - - - - - - - - - - - -

TO

106. What is: *4* ? _____

- - - - - - - - - - - - - -

AND

107. Now, try this word. *n* _____

- - - - - - - - - - - - - -

IN

108. What is this? *u* _____

- - - - - - - - - - - - - -

YOU or YOUR

109. What is this? *a* _____

- - - - - - - - - - - - - -

A

110. What is this? *4* or *f* _____

- - - - - - - - - - - - - -

FOR or FOUR

111. What is *w* ? _____

- - - - - - - - - - - - - -

WE

112. What is this? *u* _____

- - - - - - - - - - - - - -

YOUR or YOU

113. If you feel confident reading these brief forms, skip to frame 123. Otherwise, continue to review in this frame.

   What is this word? *—* _____

- - - - - - - - - - - - - -

THE

114. What is 〜 ?   _____

- - - - - - - - - - - - - -

OF

115. What is 𝟚 ?   _____

- - - - - - - - - - - - - -

TO

116. What is 𝟜 ?   _____

- - - - - - - - - - - - - -

AND

117. What is 𝓃 ?   _____

- - - - - - - - - - - - - -

IN

118. What is 𝓊 ?   _____

- - - - - - - - - - - - - -

YOU or YOUR

119. What is 𝒶 ?   _____

- - - - - - - - - - - - - -

A

120. What is 4 ?   _____

- - - - - - - - - - - - - -

FOR or FOUR

121. What is 𝓌 ?   _____

- - - - - - - - - - - - - -

WE

122. What is 𝓊 ?   _____

- - - - - - - - - - - - - -

YOU or YOUR

123. If you can read the brief forms and nothing else, you can read over
one-quarter of what is written in the office. When you add the word
beginnings and word endings that you know and the principle of writing words the way they sound, you can probably read half of every-
thing that you will see in QUICKHAND.

Shortly, you will have reading practice. But, now, try to do the
best you can in writing the brief forms. First, write THE.

124. Now, write OF.

125. Now, write TO.

126. Now, write AND.

127. Now, write IN.

128. Now, write YOU.

129. Now, write A.

130. Now, write FOR. _____

- - - - - - - - - - - - - - -

4 or *f*

131. Now, write WE. _____

- - - - - - - - - - - - -

w

132. Now, write YOUR. _____

- - - - - - - - - - - - -

u

133. You have now completed the theory of Chapter 2. Up to this point, you have studied nearly one-third of all the brief forms you will have, about one-third of all the word beginnings you will have and about half of all the word endings you will have. You have also learned the major principle of QUICKHAND, writing words the way they sound.

   In the following frames, you will be given material written in QUICKHAND. If necessary, spend a minute or two on a frame and write the material in English.

   The first QUICKHAND sentence is written below. Write the English equivalent in the answer blank provided.

   — kr km 2 — ops .

   _____

- - - - - - - - - - - - - -

THE CAR CAME TO THE OVERPASS.

134. Now, read this sentence.

   w wl h 2 k o 4 u prl .

   _____

- - - - - - - - - - - - - -

WE WILL HAVE TO COME OVER FOR YOUR PARTY.

135. Now, read this sentence.

i wl dks — mtr n a fu rs.

- - - - - - - - - - - - -

I WILL DISCUSS THE MATTER IN A FEW HOURS.

136. Now, read this sentence.

il wz a mltk 2 pt Bl & Sle 2gthr.

- - - - - - - - - - - - -

IT WAS A MISTAKE TO PUT BILL AND SALLY TOGETHER.

137. Now, read this sentence.

i wl b 1 v — akrs.

- - - - - - - - - - - - -

I WILL BE ONE OF THE ACTORS.

138. What is this sentence?

w wl nt b ab 2 ktrl — ultk.

- - - - - - - - - - - - -

WE WILL NOT BE ABLE TO CONTROL THE UNDERTAKING.

139. Now, try this sentence.

— dltkv wl nt mnng — ks v — spx hm.

- - - - - - - - - - - - -

THE DETECTIVE WILL NOT MENTION THE CASE OF THE
SPACIOUS (or SPECIAL) HOME.   (Whether you want SPACIOUS
or SPECIAL depends on the material in the rest of the article where
the sentence appears.)

140. Now, read this sentence.

— nu sm wl b plsd o — ol sky.

- - - - - - - - - - - - - - - -

THE NEW CEMENT WILL BE PLACED OVER THE OLD SECTION.

141. Don't worry if it took you a minute or two to read each frame or if
you missed a few words. If you still don't feel too confident, turn
back to frame 133 and go over the sentences again.

    Now, do the best you can in writing the sentences. Don't hesi-
tate too much if you are uncertain of a word beginning, ending, or
brief form. Just write the word the way it sounds. (Studies have
shown that if you write a word as it sounds, even if your shorthand
is not technically correct, you will very likely be able to read it
back. If you take ten or fifteen seconds to think how to write a word
correctly, you may or may not eventually get it correct; and if somebody is dictating, you are likely to miss the rest of the sentence or
the rest of the paragraph.)

    Now, write THE CAR CAME TO THE OVERPASS.

- - - - - - - - - - - - - - -

— kr km 2 — ops.

142. Remember, when writing QUICKHAND do not dot I's and J's or
cross T's. You can't afford to lose time dotting and crossing letters
that you can read anyway.

    Now, write WE WILL HAVE TO COME OVER FOR YOUR PARTY.

- - - - - - - - - - - - - - -

w wl h 2 k o 4 u prt.

143. The most important part of QUICKHAND is <u>transcription</u> or writing
back from your QUICKHAND. Don't worry if your QUICKHAND
notes don't look quite like those in the book. As long as you can
read and write back, you are doing all right. With practice, you
will learn to write correctly.

    Now, write this sentence. I WILL DISCUSS THE MATTER IN
A FEW HOURS.

- - - - - - - - - - - - - - -

i wol dks — mlr n a fu rs.

144. Now, write IT WAS A MISTAKE TO PUT BILL AND SALLY
TOGETHER.

_____

il wz a mlk 2 pl Bl ∂ Sle 2glhr.

145. Write this sentence. I WILL BE ONE OF THE ACTORS.

_____

i wol b 1 v — akrs.

(Remember the CT in ACTORS is written the way it sounds, with a
k .)

146. Now, write WE WILL NOT BE ABLE TO CONTROL THE UNDER-
TAKING.

_____

w wol nl b ab 2 klrl — ulk..

147. Now, write THE DETECTIVE WILL NOT MENTION THE CASE
OF THE SPACIOUS HOME.

_____

— dlkv wol nl mng — ks v — spx hm.

148. Write THE NEW CEMENT WILL BE PLACED OVER THE OLD
SECTION.

_____

— nu sm wol b plsd o — ol sky.

You have now had a chance to read and to write material repre-
senting every principle, word beginning, word ending, and brief form
you have covered up to this point. Don't worry if your writing is going

slowly and if you struggle with your reading. You will have plenty of opportunity to practice what you have learned, without memorization or direct repetition, in the next chapters.

If you want immediate review, turn to frame 141 to practice writing or to frame 133 to practice reading. But this time, go over the material quickly. You will review the material in the next chapters while you are also covering new material.

If you are not reviewing, go on to the Self-Test for this chapter.

SELF-TEST

A. Write the following words in QUICKHAND.

(1) MIDDLE _____   (5) MENTION _____

(2) COMPARE _____   (6) YOU _____

(3) OVERPASS _____   (7) OF _____

(4) TABLE _____

B. Transcribe the following words.

(1) *kbrl* _____   (4) *—* _____

(2) *ups* _____   (5) *q* _____

(3) *ulk.* _____

C. Write the following sentences in QUICKHAND.

(1) I ADMIT IT WAS A MISTAKE TO PUT BILL AND SALLY

TOGETHER. _____

(2) THE CAR CAME TO THE OVERPASS.

_____

D. Transcribe the following sentences.

(1) *— nu sm wl b plad o — ol sky.*

_____

(2) *w wl h 2 k o 4 u prl.*

_____

E. Write the following sentences (which you have not had in this chapter).

(1) WE GOT A NEW CAR TODAY!

_____

(2) THE DEAL WAS OFF WHEN HE FORGOT TO GET THE LETTER.

_____

(3) I AM SORRY WE WILL NOT SEE YOU LATER.

_____

F. Transcribe the following sentences (which you have not had in this chapter).

(1) *nr krs i wvl b al u prl!*

_____

(2) *plz km 2 — hs wn — ml. z o.*

_____

(3) *wn wvl u b ab 2 k o 2 br. — nu edj?*

_____

Answers

A. (1) *mdl* ; (2) *kpr* ; (3) *ops* ; (4) *lb* ;
    (5) *mny* ; (6) *u* ; (7) *nr*

B. (1) CONTROL; (2) UNDERPASS; (3) UNDERTAKING; (4) THE;
    (5) AND

C. (1) *i adml il wz a mlk 2 pl Bl & Sle 2glhr.*
    (2) *— hr km 2 — ops.*

D. (1) THE NEW CEMENT WILL BE PLACED OVER THE OLD SECTION.
    (2) WE WILL HAVE TO COME OVER FOR YOUR PARTY.

E. (1) *w gl a nu kr 2da!*
    (2) *— dl wz of wn he 4gl 2 gl — llr.*
    (3) *i am sre w wvl nl c u llr.*

F. (1) OF COURSE I WILL BE AT YOUR PARTY!
    (2) PLEASE COME TO THE HOUSE WHEN THE MEETING IS OVER.
    (3) WHEN WILL YOU BE ABLE TO COME OVER TO BRING THE
         NEW EDITION?

If you would like additional practice before you start the next chapter, turn to the Supplemental Exercise for this chapter in the back of the book.

Chapter Three

1. In this chapter, you will cover the second group of word beginnings (there will be one more group in the succeeding lesson), the second and last group of word endings, and the eleventh through twentieth brief forms. (There will be a total of thirty-five.)

   Let's start with word beginnings. The words TRANSACT and TRANSIT are written below.

   lak ll

   Can you tell how TRANS is written? _____

   - - - - - - - - - - - - - - - - -

   TRANS is written with *l* .

2. What is this word? *lfr* _____

   - - - - - - - - - - - - - - - - -

   TRANSFER

3. What is this? *lprl* _____

   - - - - - - - - - - - - - - - - -

   TRANSPORT

4. What is this word? *lprly* _____

   - - - - - - - - - - - - - - - - -

   TRANSPORTATION

5. Do you want to guess how UN is written? UNTIL is written this way:

   nll   How do you think the UN is written? _____

   - - - - - - - - - - - - - - - - - - -

UN is written *n* .

6.   What is this word? *ndrs*   _____

- - - - - - - - - - - - - -

UNDRESS (or ENDORSE)

7.   What is this word? *nnrv*   _____

- - - - - - - - - - - - - -

UNNERVE

8.   What is this word? *nfl.*   _____

- - - - - - - - - - - - - -

UNFEELING

9.   The words ENTERTAIN and INTERACT are written below.

nln   *nak*   Can you tell how the ENTER and INTER word

beginnings are written?   _____

- - - - - - - - - - - - - -

n

10. The ENTER and INTER sounds are also written with *n* . Of
     course, you can tell whether you mean UN, ENTER, or INTER by
     the way the word is used in the sentence.

     Can you read this word? *nln*   _____

- - - - - - - - - - - - - -

ENTERTAIN

11. What is this word? *njk*   _____

- - - - - - - - - - - - - -

INTERJECT

12. What is this word? *nsky*   `   _____

- - - - - - - - - - - - - -

INTERSECTION

13. What is this word? *nrp* _____

- - - - - - - - - - - - - - -

INTERRUPT

14. The words CIRCLE, CIRCUMFERENCE, and CIRCULAR are written below.

    cl cfrns clr   Can you tell how the CIRC, CIRCU,

    and CIRCUM word beginnings are written? _____

- - - - - - - - - - - - - - -

    CIRC, CIRCU, and CIRCUM are written *c* .

15. What is this word? *cslns* _____

- - - - - - - - - - - - - - -

    CIRCUMSTANCE

16. What is this word? *clj* _____

- - - - - - - - - - - - - - -

    CIRCULATION

17. What is this word? *clrj* _____

- - - - - - - - - - - - - - -

    CIRCULARIZE

18. In the English language, there are a few sounds that can be either word beginnings or word endings. Look at the words below to see if you can name two of these sounds.

    CARRY, REWARD _____

    EARFUL, FULFILL _____

- - - - - - - - - - - - - - -

    The RE and FULL sounds can be both word beginnings and word endings. Remember, in QUICKHAND be concerned with the way words sound and not the way they are spelled. The beginning RE is spelled RE while the ending is usually spelled RY.

19. How do you think the beginning RE is written? The words RECALL and REWARD are written below.

    rkl   rwrd

    How do you think the RE is written? _____

    - - - - - - - - - - - - - - -

    The RE is written *r* .

20. What is this word? *rml* _____

    - - - - - - - - - - - - - - -

    REMIT

21. What is this word? *rgrl* _____

    - - - - - - - - - - - - - - -

    REGRET

22. What is this word? *rgrs* _____

    - - - - - - - - - - - - - - -

    REGRESS

23. Remembering that in QUICKHAND you write according to sound, if the word beginning RE is written with an *r* , how do you think the word ending RY is written? _____

    - - - - - - - - - - - - - - -

    The word ending RY is also written with an *r* . It sounds the same as the word beginning RE so it is written the same way.

24. Can you read this word? *kr* _____

    - - - - - - - - - - - - - - -

    CARRY (or CAR)

25. What is this word? *mr* _____

    - - - - - - - - - - - - - - -

    MARRY (or MAR)

26. Can you tell what these names are? *Kr   Mr*

_____

- - - - - - - - - - - - - - - -

CARRIE, MARY

27. Do you want to guess how the word beginning FUL is written in the
QUICKHAND Shorthand System? The words FULLER and FULLY
are written below.

flr   fle

Can you tell how FUL is written? _____

- - - - - - - - - - - - - - - -

FUL is written *f* .

28. What is this word? *ff* _____

- - - - - - - - - - - - - - - -

FULFILL

29. There you see that the word endings FILL and FUL are written

f . What is this word? *krf* _____

- - - - - - - - - - - - - - - -

CAREFUL

30. What is this word? *rlf* _____

- - - - - - - - - - - - - - - -

RIGHTFUL

31. What is this word? *fglf* _____

- - - - - - - - - - - - - - - -

FORGETFUL

32. With the RE and the FUL, you have completed the second group of
word beginnings. You have also begun to study the last group of word
endings. Before covering more word endings, let's review the material we just covered in this chapter.

What is this word? _𝓊_ _____

- - - - - - - - - - - - - -

TRANSIT

33. What is this word? _nls_ _____

- - - - - - - - - - - - - -

UNLESS

34. What is this word? _nln_ _____

- - - - - - - - - - - - - -

ENTERTAIN

35. What is this word? _nsl_ _____

- - - - - - - - - - - - - -

INTEREST (or NEST)

36. What is this word? _cl_ _____

- - - - - - - - - - - - - -

CIRCLE

37. What is this word? _clr_ _____

- - - - - - - - - - - - - -

CIRCULAR

38. What is this word? _cslns_ _____

- - - - - - - - - - - - - -

CIRCUMSTANCE

39. What is this word? _rwrd_ _____

- - - - - - - - - - - - - -

REWARD

40. What is this word? *if* _____

- - - - - - - - - - - - -

EYEFUL

41. Now, let's write some words in QUICKHAND. First, write TRANSIT. _____

- - - - - - - - - - - - - -

u

42. Now, write UNLESS. _____

- - - - - - - - - - - - -

nls

43. Now, write ENTERTAIN. _____

- - - - - - - - - - - - -

ntn

44. Now, write INTEREST. _____

- - - - - - - - - - - - -

nst

45. Now, write CIRCLE. _____

- - - - - - - - - - - - -

cl

46. Now, write CIRCULAR. _____

- - - - - - - - - - - - -

clr

47. Now, write CIRCUMSTANCE. _____

- - - - - - - - - - - - -

cstns

48. Now, write REWARD. _____

- - - - - - - - - - - - - -

rurd

49. Now, write EYEFUL. _____

- - - - - - - - - - - - - -

if

50. If you want to review writing word beginnings, turn back to frame
41. Otherwise, continue with this frame.

The word LOWLY is written *lol* . How do you think the LY

is written? _____

- - - - - - - - - - - - - -

The LY is written *l* .

51. What is this word? *slol* _____

- - - - - - - - - - - - - -

SLOWLY

52. What is this word? *hil* _____

- - - - - - - - - - - - - -

HIGHLY or HILLY

53. The ANCE and ENCE word endings are frequently used in English.
They are represented with two letters. Can you tell from the words
GLANCE and SENSE below how these word endings are written?

glns sns _____

- - - - - - - - - - - - - -

The ANCE and ENCE are written *ns* .

54. What is this word? *cslns* _____

- - - - - - - - - - - - - -

CIRCUMSTANCE

55. What is this word? *nnsns* _____

- - - - - - - - - - - - - - - -

NONSENSE

56. What is this word? *fns* _____

- - - - - - - - - - - - - - - -

FENCE

57. The last two word endings to be covered are WARD and HOOD.
TOWARD and MANHOOD are written below. How do you write
WARD and HOOD?

lwd   mnhd

WARD: _____   HOOD: _____

- - - - - - - - - - - - - - - -

WARD is written *wd* ; HOOD is written *hd* .

58. What is this word? *lwd* _____

- - - - - - - - - - - - - - - -

TOWARD

59. What is this word? *rwd* _____

- - - - - - - - - - - - - - - -

REWARD

60. What is this word? *mlhrhd* _____

- - - - - - - - - - - - - - - -

MOTHERHOOD

61. You have now studied all of the word endings you will have. Let's
review the ones covered in this lesson.

    What is this word? *kr* _____

- - - - - - - - - - - - - - - -

CARRY

62. What is this word? *rf* _____

- - - - - - - - - - - - -

EARFUL or REFILL

63. What is this word? *cfrns* _____

- - - - - - - - - - - - -

CIRCUMFERENCE

64. What is this word? *krfl* _____

- - - - - - - - - - - - -

CAREFULLY

65. What is this word? *snlns* _____

- - - - - - - - - - - - -

SENTENCE

66. What is this word? *fwd* _____

- - - - - - - - - - - - -

FORWARD

67. What is this word? *mnhd* _____

- - - - - - - - - - - - -

MANHOOD

68. Now, let's write some words with these endings. First, write
TARRY. _____

- - - - - - - - - - - - -

lr

69. Now, write EARFUL. _____

- - - - - - - - - - - - -

rf

70. Now, write CIRCUMFERENCE.   _____

- - - - - - - - - - - - - -

cfrns

71. Now, write CAREFULLY.   _____

- - - - - - - - - - - - - -

krfl

72. Now, write SENTENCE.   _____

- - - - - - - - - - - - - -

snlns

73. Now, write FORWARD.   _____

- - - - - - - - - - - - - -

frwd   or   *fwd*

74. Now, write MANHOOD.   _____

- - - - - - - - - - - - - -

mnhd

75. You have now completed the study of word endings. Notice that many words are made up of several word beginnings and endings which can be abbreviated in QUICKHAND with one letter. When you combine beginnings and endings in the same word, you can write QUICKHAND very easily.

   You will now study ten more brief forms (words eleven through twenty in the frequency of use in office correspondence.)

   Word number eleven is THAT. How do you think you write it in

QUICKHAND?   _____

- - - - - - - - - - - - - -

THAT is written *ʟ* .

76. Word number twelve is THIS. How do you think THIS is written?

   _____

- - - - - - - - - - - - - -

THIS is written *ᴧ* .

77. The next word, number thirteen, is BE. How do you think you write

    BE? _____

    - - - - - - - - - - - - - -

    BE is written *ℓ* .

78. Word fourteen is IS. It is written with its dominant sound. How do

    you write IS? _____

    - - - - - - - - - - - - - -

    ȝ

79. Word fifteen is I. Do you know how to write I? _____

    - - - - - - - - - - - - - -

    I is written *ᴧ* , without the dot.

80. The next word, number sixteen, is OUR. You should know how to

    write it. How do you think you write OUR? _____

    - - - - - - - - - - - - - -

    OUR is *ᴧ* .

81. Word seventeen is WILL. It is written with the last letter. How do

    you think you write WILL? _____

    - - - - - - - - - - - - - -

    WILL is written *ℓ* .

82. Word eighteen is HAVE. It is written with one letter. How do you

    think you write HAVE? _____

    - - - - - - - - - - - - - -

    HAVE is written *ℏ* .

83. The next word, number nineteen, is ON. It is written with the last

    letter. Try writing ON. _____

    - - - - - - - - - - - - - - - - - - -

ON is written 𝓃 .

84. Word twenty is WITH. It is written with the first letter. Try writing
WITH. _____

- - - - - - - - - - - - - - -

WITH is written 𝓊𝓇 .

85. In the next frames, do the best you can in reading the new brief
forms. Don't spend too much time on them now, as you will have
much more time to read them in sentences, where they will make
more sense, in the exercises at the end of this chapter.

What is this word? 𝓁   _____

- - - - - - - - - - - - - - -

THAT

86. What is 𝒶 ? _____

- - - - - - - - - - - - - - -

THIS

87. What is 𝒷 ? _____

- - - - - - - - - - - - - - -

BE

88. What is 𝓎 ? _____

- - - - - - - - - - - - - - -

IS (or AS)

89. What is 𝓁 ? _____

- - - - - - - - - - - - - - -

I

90. What is this word? 𝓇   _____

- - - - - - - - - - - - - - -

OUR (or ARE, HOUR, OR)

91. What is *ℓ* ?   _____

- - - - - - - - - - - - - - -

WILL

92. What is this word? *h*   _____

- - - - - - - - - - - - - - -

HAVE

93. What is *n* ?   _____

- - - - - - - - - - - - - - -

ON (or IN)

94. What is *w* ?   _____

- - - - - - - - - - - - - - -

WITH

95. If you want to read these words once more, proceed with this frame. If you don't think it is necessary to read them again, skip to frame 105.

What is this word? *L*   _____

- - - - - - - - - - - - - - -

THAT

96. What is *s* ?   _____

- - - - - - - - - - - - - - -

THIS

97. What is this word? *b*   _____

- - - - - - - - - - - - - - -

BE

98. What is this word? *z*   _____

- - - - - - - - - - - - - - -

IS (or AS)

99. What is *ι* ? _____

- - - - - - - - - - - - - - -

I

100. What is *η* ? _____

- - - - - - - - - - - - - - -

OUR (or ARE, HOUR, OR)

101. What is *ℓ* ? _____

- - - - - - - - - - - - - - -

WILL

102. What is *h* ? _____

- - - - - - - - - - - - - - -

HAVE

103. What is *n* ? _____

- - - - - - - - - - - - - - -

ON (or IN)

104. What is *w* ? _____

- - - - - - - - - - - - - - -

WITH

105. You will have more opportunity to read these words in the exercises at the end of this chapter. Now you will have an opportunity to write the new brief forms. See how well you do.

First, write THAT. _____

- - - - - - - - - - - - - -

ι

106. Now, write THIS. _____

- - - - - - - - - - - - - -

ρ

107. Now, write BE. _____

- - - - - - - - - - - - - -

b

108. Now, write IS. _____

- - - - - - - - - - - - - -

z

109. Now, write I. _____

- - - - - - - - - - - - - -

ι

110. Now, write OUR. _____

- - - - - - - - - - - - - -

r

111. Now, write WILL. _____

- - - - - - - - - - - - - -

l

112. Now, write HAVE. _____

- - - - - - - - - - - - - -

h

113. Now, write ON. _____

- - - - - - - - - - - - - -

n

114. Now, write WITH. _____

- - - - - - - - - - - - - -

w

115. If you want to practice writing these brief forms again, turn back to frame 105. But don't dwell on the writing of brief forms now. You will soon have a chance to use all of them in sentences.

    In the next frames, you will be given sentences to read. Do the best you can. If you can't make out a word, see if you can understand the rest of the sentence and then fill in the word. If necessary, spend a minute or two on each frame. When you think you can read the sentence, or you have tried to read it and can't make it out, check the English in the answer.

    The sentence below contains several brief forms. Write out the English.

    z l ma b ll, s l b r lsl gm.

- - - - - - - - - - - - - - -

    AS IT MAY BE LATE, THIS WILL BE OUR LAST GAME.

116. How did you do? If you couldn't quite make it out, look back to see if you can understand it now. Once you understand the sentence, try another one.

    The sentence below also contains examples of many principles covered in Chapter 3. When you have done the best you can, check your answer.

    he z go. 2 tprt — dlvr.

- - - - - - - - - - - - - - -

    HE IS GOING TO TRANSPORT THE DELIVERY.

117. If you didn't quite read it correctly, does it make sense when you go back to look at it? As soon as it seems to make sense, try the sentence below.

    w r go. 2 wt ntll he ffz hz prms.*

- - - - - - - - - - - - - - -

    WE ARE GOING TO WAIT UNTIL HE FULFILLS HIS PROMISE.

---

*You may write the "z" sound, as in *"fulfills"* and *"his"* with either the s or the z. In the remainder of this book, it is generally written with the "z."

118. Do the best you can with the sentence below, then check the answer.

un w h — lslr rdo m, w hr m rf.

- - - - - - - - - - - - - - -

WHEN WE HAVE THE TRANSISTOR RADIO ON, WE HEAR AN EARFUL.

119. Are the sentences making sense when you go back to compare the QUICKHAND with the English? Try another one.

he l mds hr 2 hz cl v frnz.

- - - - - - - - - - - - - - -

HE WILL INTRODUCE HER TO HIS CIRCLE OF FRIENDS.

120. Try this one.

Hr l rml — pam twd — nd v — wk.

- - - - - - - - - - - - - - -

HARRY WILL REMIT THE PAYMENT TOWARD THE END OF THE WEEK.

121. When you have finished with this sentence, check your answer.

she l rt hr krspndns 2 hr frnz m — nbrhd.

- - - - - - - - - - - - - - -

SHE WILL WRITE HER CORRESPONDENCE TO HER FRIENDS IN THE NEIGHBORHOOD.

122. Write the English translation for this one.

he flz 2 rt ppl m — flr lns.

- - - - - - - - - - - - - - -

HE FAILS TO WRITE PROPERLY IN THE FUTURE TENSE.

123. Do your best with this last sentence.

he l rdl agre l l z n yf.

- - - - - - - - - - - - -

HE WILL READILY AGREE THAT IT IS AN EYEFUL.

124. If you wish, you may turn back to frame 115 to read the sentences again. Otherwise, try to write some complete sentences in QUICKHAND in the next few frames.

First write AS IT MAY BE LATE, THIS WILL BE OUR LAST GAME.

- - - - - - - - - - - - - -

z l ma b ll, s l b r lsl gm.

125. Now, write HE IS GOING TO TRANSPORT THE DELIVERY.

- - - - - - - - - - - - -

he z go. 2 spl — dlvr.

126. Now, write WE ARE GOING TO WAIT UNTIL HE FULFILLS HIS PROMISE.

- - - - - - - - - - - - -

w r go. 2 wl nll he ffz hz prms.

127. Now, write WHEN WE HAVE THE TRANSISTOR RADIO ON, WE HEAR AN EARFUL.

- - - - - - - - - - - - -

wn w h - lslr rdo n, w hr n rf.

128. Now, write HE WILL INTRODUCE HER TO HIS CIRCLE OF FRIENDS.

- - - - - - - - - - - - -

he l nds hr 2 hz cl v frnz.

129. Now, write HARRY WILL REMIT THE PAYMENT TOWARD THE END OF THE WEEK.

Hr l rml — pam lwd — nd v — wk.

130. Try SHE WILL WRITE HER CORRESPONDENCE TO HER FRIENDS IN THE NEIGHBORHOOD.

---

she l rt hr krspndns 2 hr frz n — nbrhd.

131. Now, write HE FAILS TO WRITE PROPERLY IN THE FUTURE TENSE.

---

he flz 2 rt ppl n — flr lns.

132. Now, write HE WILL READILY AGREE THAT IT IS AN EYEFUL.

---

he l rdl agre l l z n if.

133. If you want to review reading QUICKHAND, turn back to frame 115. If you want to review writing, turn back to frame 124. Otherwise, read the following QUICKHAND message.

s kkldz chplr 3.

The message says THIS CONCLUDES CHAPTER THREE. What does the sentence below say?

go 2 — slf lst wch floz.

It says GO TO THE SELF-TEST WHICH FOLLOWS.

SELF-TEST

A. Write the following words in QUICKHAND.

  (1) SENSE _____   (5) BE _____

  (2) DEARLY _____   (6) ON _____

  (3) FULFILL _____   (7) ENACT _____

  (4) BACKWARD _____

B. Transcribe the following words.

  (1) *fns* _____   (5) *s* _____

  (2) *gls* _____   (6) *h* _____

  (3) *fwd* _____   (7) *nbrhd* _____

  (4) *mnhd* _____

C. Write the following sentences in QUICKHAND.

  (1) WE ARE GOING TO WAIT UNTIL HE FULFILLS HIS PROMISE.

  _____

  (2) HE WILL INTRODUCE HER TO HIS CIRCLE OF FRIENDS.

  _____

D. Transcribe the following sentences.

  (1) *Hr l rml — pam lwd — nd r — wrk.*

  _____

  (2) *he z go. 2 sprl — dlr.*

  _____

E. Write the following sentences (which you have not had before).

  (1) THIS WILL BE THE LAST WARNING.

  _____

  (2) HE IS HAPPY TO BE IN SCHOOL.

  _____

F. Transcribe the following sentences (which you have not had before).

(1) *w l h 2 wl 4 — rspns bf w tk akj.*

(2) *w l h ntnm al — prt.*

Answers

A. (1) *sns* ; (2) *drl* ; (3) *ff* ; (4) *bkwd* ;
    (5) *b* ; (6) *n* ; (7) *mak*

B. (1) FENCE; (2) GLASS; (3) FORWARD; (4) MANHOOD; (5) THIS;
    (6) HAVE; (7) NEIGHBORHOOD

C. (1) *w r go. 2 wl nll he ffz hz prms.*
    (2) *he l nds hr 2 hz cl r frnz.*

D. (1) HARRY WILL REMIT THE PAYMENT TOWARD THE END OF
        THE WEEK.
    (2) HE IS GOING TO TRANSPORT THE DELIVERY.

E. (1) *a l b — lst wrn. .*
    (2) *he z hp 2 b n skl.*

F. (1) WE WILL HAVE TO WAIT FOR THE RESPONSE BEFORE WE
        TAKE ACTION.
    (2) WE WILL HAVE ENTERTAINMENT AT THE PARTY.

If you would like additional practice before you start the next chapter, turn to the Supplemental Exercise for this chapter in the back of the book.

Chapter Four

1. In Chapter 4, you will learn how to form the past tense and how to
    use standard abbreviations (which you probably know already). You
    will also have the last group of word beginnings and nine more BRIEF
    FORMS.

    We will start with the past tense in the QUICKHAND Shorthand
    System. For irregular verbs, just <u>write the past tense the way it
    sounds</u>.

    Try a few examples. Write MISTOOK. _____

    - - - - - - - - - - - - - - - -

    mltk

2. Write SAID. _____

    - - - - - - - - - - - - - - - -

    sd

3. Write WENT. _____

    - - - - - - - - - - - - - - - -

    wnt

4. Write RAN. _____

    - - - - - - - - - - - - - - - -

    rn

5. For regular verbs, when you add an ED or a D to the English word to
    form the past tense, just underline the last letter of the QUICKHAND
    word to make the past tense. For example, look at the words JUMP
    and JUMPED in QUICKHAND on the following page.

ymp   ymp

Now, you will have a chance to write regular verbs and their past tense. Write: DISCUSS and DISCUSSED. _____

- - - - - - - - - - - - - - - -

dks   dks

6. Now, write DRILL and DRILLED. _____

- - - - - - - - - - - - - - - -

drl   drl

7. When you write the QUICKHAND Shorthand System, use any standard abbreviations with which you are familiar. If you know that there is a standard abbreviation, but are not sure what it is, use your own abbreviation if you can read it back. Otherwise, write the way a word sounds.

You probably know many of the standard abbreviations in the following frames. Let's see just how many you do know. But don't be concerned if there are some that you don't know.

Do you recognize this abbreviation? *co.* _____

- - - - - - - - - - - - - - -

COMPANY

8. How about this one? *govt.* _____

- - - - - - - - - - - - - - -

GOVERNMENT

9. Do you know this one? **IRS** _____

- - - - - - - - - - - - - - -

INTERNAL REVENUE SERVICE

10. What is this abbreviation? **RR** _____

- - - - - - - - - - - - - - -

RAILROAD

11. How about this one? *inc.* _____

- - - - - - - - - - - - - -

INCORPORATED

12. How about this abbreviation? *mgr.* _____

- - - - - - - - - - - - - -

MANAGER

13. What is this? *"* _____

- - - - - - - - - - - - - -

INCHES

14. Do you recognize this standard abbreviation? *'* _____

- - - - - - - - - - - - - -

FEET

15. How about this one? *@* _____

- - - - - - - - - - - - - -

AT

16. What is this? *p/l* _____

- - - - - - - - - - - - - -

PRICE LIST

17. What is this? *o/a* _____

- - - - - - - - - - - - - -

ON ACCOUNT

18. What is this? *esl.* _____

- - - - - - - - - - - - - -

ESTABLISHED

19. What is this abbreviation? *EST* _____

- - - - - - - - - - - - - -

EASTERN STANDARD TIME

20. Did you recognize most of these abbreviations? Again, if there are some you don't know, don't use them.

There are many more standard abbreviations. Use any that you know.

<u>Proper names</u> are very important. In writing back from your QUICKHAND notes, if you spell a person's name incorrectly, it may cost your organization greatly. However, when you write in QUICK-HAND Shorthand, don't worry about the spelling of names. Abbreviate them informally: Bill Jones can be BJ; Jim Smith can be JS. When you are on the job, ask the person dictating to tell you all the names he or she will give you before dictation begins. Then write them in longhand so you will have them when it comes time to write in English.

u kn rd & rl a grl dl n kwkhnd. go n now 2 lrn r lsl grp r wrd bgn.z.

That message said YOU CAN READ AND WRITE A GREAT DEAL IN QUICKHAND. GO ON NOW TO LEARN OUR LAST GROUP OF WORD BEGINNINGS.

Many words in English start with FAR, FIR, FOR, and FUR. Do you think you know how these word beginnings are written? If so, skip to frame 21. Otherwise, read on.

The words FARMER and FOREMAN are written below.

fmr   *fmn*

Can you tell how the FAR, FIR, FOR, and FUR sounds are written?

_____

- - - - - - - - - - - - - -

The word beginnings FAR, FIR, FOR, and FUR are written *f* .

21. Can you read this word? *fll* _____

- - - - - - - - - - - - - -

FORETELL

22. What is this word? *flhr* _____

- - - - - - - - - - - - - -

FARTHER or FURTHER

23. What is this word?   *fm*   _____

- - - - - - - - - - - - - - -

FARM, FIRM, or FORM

24. Other frequently used word beginnings are MAN, MEN, MIN, and

MON. Can you guess how they are written? Try it here. _____
   The words MENTAL and MINIMUM are written below.

   mll   *mmm*

Can you tell now how the MAN, MEN, MIN, and MON sounds are

written?   _____

- - - - - - - - - - - - - - -

The MAN, MEN, MIN, and MON sounds are written *m* .

25. Can you read this word? *mdl*   _____

- - - - - - - - - - - - - - -

MANDATE

26. How about this word? *me*   _____

- - - - - - - - - - - - - - -

MONEY or MANY

27. Other frequently used word beginnings are the PRE and PRO sounds.

Can you guess how these are written? Try it here.   _____
   The words PREFIX and PROJECT are written below.

   pfx *pjk*

Can you tell how the PRE and PRO sounds are written?

_____

- - - - - - - - - - - - - - -

The PRE and PRO are written *p* .

28. What is this word? *pfm*   _____

- - - - - - - - - - - - - - -

PERFORM

29. What is this word? *ppr* _____

- - - - - - - - - - - - -

PROPER, PREPARE (or PAPER)

30. The word beginnings COUNTER and CONTRA are very long. Yet, in QUICKHAND, you can write them with one letter. Do you think you know how to write these word beginnings? How about trying it here?

_____.

The words COUNTERACT and CONTRADICT are written below.

kak   kdk

Can you tell now how COUNTER and CONTRA are written?

_____.

- - - - - - - - - - - - - -

The COUNTER and CONTRA are written *k* , the same as the COM and CON. Of course, you can tell which sound you want by what makes sense.

31. What is this word? *kof* _____

- - - - - - - - - - - - - -

COUNTEROFFER

32. What is this word? *kdky* _____

- - - - - - - - - - - - - -

CONTRADICTION

33. What is this word? *klbnd* _____

- - - - - - - - - - - - - -

CONTRABAND

34. The last word beginnings you will study are the SUB and SIR sounds.

If you want, guess how these sounds are written. _____
The words SUBSIDE and SURVEY are written below.

ssd   sva

Can you show how the SUB and SIR sounds are written?

_____

- - - - - - - - - - - - - - - -

SUB and SIR are written *s* .

35. What is *ssd* ? _____

- - - - - - - - - - - - - - - -

SUBSIDE or SUBSIDY

36. What is this word? *sml* _____

- - - - - - - - - - - - - - - -

SUBMIT

37. What is this word? *sdvd* _____

- - - - - - - - - - - - - - - -

SUBDIVIDE

38. What is this word? *sva* _____

- - - - - - - - - - - - - - - -

SURVEY

39. Before going on, let's review the word beginnings you have just learned by reading some words with them.

What is this word? *fmr* _____

- - - - - - - - - - - - - - - -

FARMER, FORMER, or FIRMER

40. What is this word? *mr* _____

- - - - - - - - - - - - - - - -

MANOR (or MARRY)

41. What is this word? *ppr* _____

- - - - - - - - - - - - - - - -

PROPER, PREPARE (or PAPER)

42. What is this word? *pvd* _____

- - - - - - - - - - - - - - -

PROVIDE

43. What is this word? *kak* _____

- - - - - - - - - - - - - - -

COUNTERACT

44. What is this? *sssl* _____

- - - - - - - - - - - - - - -

SUBSIST

45. What is this word? *sfe* _____

- - - - - - - - - - - - - - -

SURFACE

46. If you want to review the last group of word beginnings again, turn back to frame 20. Otherwise, go on to write words with these word beginnings.

First, write FARMER. _____

- - - - - - - - - - - - - - -

fmr

47. Now, write MANOR. _____

- - - - - - - - - - - - - - -

mr

48. Now, write PREPARE. _____

- - - - - - - - - - - - - - -

ppr

49. Now, write PROVIDE. _____

- - - - - - - - - - - - - -

pvd

50. Next, write COUNTERACT. _____

- - - - - - - - - - - - - -

kak

51. Now, write SUBSIST. _____

- - - - - - - - - - - - - -

ssst

52. Next, write SURFACE. _____

- - - - - - - - - - - - - -

sfa

53. If you want to review writing these words, turn back to frame 46. In the rest of this lesson, you will learn nine more brief forms (words twenty-one through twenty-nine in frequency of use in the office).

Word number twenty-one is ARE. Do you know how to write ARE?

_____

- - - - - - - - - - - - - -

ARE is written *ʌ* .

54. The next word is AS. Can you tell how to write AS? _____

- - - - - - - - - - - - - -

AS is written *z* .

55. The next word, number twenty-three, is IT. It is written with the last letter. How do you write IT? _____

- - - - - - - - - - - - - -

IT is written *l* .

56. The word following IT is AT. Can you write AT? _____

- - - - - - - - - - - - - -

AT is written with the standard abbreviation *@* .

57. The next word, number twenty-five, is WOULD. Do you know how to write WOULD? _____

- - - - - - - - - - - - - -

WOULD is written *wd* .

58. The next word, number twenty-six, is BY. It is written with the first letter. Write BY. _____

- - - - - - - - - - - - - -

BY is written *b* .

59. The twenty-seventh form is NOT. It is written with the first letter. Do you know how to write NOT? _____

- - - - - - - - - - - - - -

NOT is written *n* .

60. Word twenty-eight is WHICH. It is written with two letters. Do you know how to write WHICH? _____

- - - - - - - - - - - - - -

WHICH is written *wc* . (You will see later how the C represents the CH sound.)

61. Brief form twenty-nine, the last to be covered in this lesson, is IF. It is written with the last letter. Do you know how to write IF?

_____

- - - - - - - - - - - - - -

IF is written *f* .

62. In the next frames, you will have an opportunity to recognize these new brief forms.

Can you read this new brief form? r ____________________

- - - - - - - - - - - - - - - -

ARE (or OUR, HOUR, OR)

63. What is this word? z ____________________

- - - - - - - - - - - - - - - -

AS (or IS)

64. What is this word? t ____________________

- - - - - - - - - - - - - - - -

IT (or THAT)

65. What is this word? @ ____________________

- - - - - - - - - - - - - - - -

AT

66. What is this word? wd ____________________

- - - - - - - - - - - - - - - -

WOULD (or WOOD)

67. What is this word? b ____________________

- - - - - - - - - - - - - - - -

BY (or BE)

68. What is this word? n ____________________

- - - - - - - - - - - - - - - -

NOT (or IN or ON)

69. What is this word? wc ____________________

- - - - - - - - - - - - - - - -

WHICH

70. What is this word? _f_ _____

- - - - - - - - - - - - - - -

IF (or FOR or FOUR)

71. If you are confident in reading these new brief forms, skip to frame 80. Otherwise, read them once more.

Can you read this word? _r_ _____

- - - - - - - - - - - - - - -

ARE (or OUR, HOUR, OR)

72. What is this word? _z_ _____

- - - - - - - - - - - - - - -

AS (or IS)

73. What is _l_ ? _____

- - - - - - - - - - - - - - -

IT (or THAT)

74. What is this word? _@_ _____

- - - - - - - - - - - - - - -

AT

75. What is this word? _wd_ _____

- - - - - - - - - - - - - - -

WOULD (or WOOD)

76. What is this word? _b_ _____

- - - - - - - - - - - - - - -

BY (or BE)

77. What is this word? _n_ _____

- - - - - - - - - - - - - - -

NOT (or IN or ON)

78. What is this word? *wc* _____

- - - - - - - - - - - - - - -

WHICH

79. What is this word? *f* _____

- - - - - - - - - - - - - - -

IF (or FOR or FOUR)

80. You will now have an opportunity to write each of the new brief forms in this chapter. First, write ARE. Check your QUICKHAND against that in the answer. _____

- - - - - - - - - - - - - - -

r

81. Now, write AS. _____

- - - - - - - - - - - - - - -

z

82. Now, write IT. _____

- - - - - - - - - - - - - - -

l

83. Now, write AT. _____

- - - - - - - - - - - - - - -

@

84. Now, write WOULD. _____

- - - - - - - - - - - - - - -

wd

85. Now, write BY. _____

- - - - - - - - - - - - - - -

b

86. Now, write NOT. _____

- - - - - - - - - - - - - -

n

87. Now, write WHICH. _____

- - - - - - - - - - - -

wc

88. Now, write IF. _____

- - - - - - - - - - - - - -

f

89. You will have an opportunity to read and write these new brief forms in meaningful sentences in the exercises which follow. If, however, you want to practice writing them once more before you begin the exercises, turn back to frame 80.

In the exercises, you will have an opportunity to review all of the principles and brief forms covered up to this point.

Try reading this sentence. *ı blv ł he z n w ł.*

_____

- - - - - - - - - - - - - - -

I BELIEVE THAT HE IS NOT WITH IT.

90. If you had difficulty with that sentence (or with any others in these exercises) look again at the QUICKHAND Shorthand and see if the sentence makes sense after you have seen it in English.

Now, try reading this. *he l rsv hz rpl ৮ Ocl 9.*

_____

- - - - - - - - - - - - - - -

HE WILL RECEIVE HIS REPLY BY OCTOBER 9.

91. Try reading this. *pl ll r erm wc bk u pln 2 rzv @ − lbrr.*

_____

- - - - - - - - - - - - - - -

PLEASE TELL OUR CHAIRMAN WHICH BOOK YOU PLAN TO
RESERVE AT THE LIBRARY.

92. Try this sentence. — *kmdr pd — bl @ — str.*

— — — — — — — — — — — — — — — — —

THE COMMANDER PAID THE BILL AT THE STORE.

93. What is this sentence? *hz fmr wf wd n pml hm 2 c hz sn.*

— — — — — — — — — — — — — — — — —

HIS FORMER WIFE WOULD NOT PERMIT HIM TO SEE HIS SON.

94. Now, read this. — *jj rl̲ n — mll kdy v — dfndnt.*

— — — — — — — — — — — — — — — — —

THE JUDGE RULED ON THE MENTAL CONDITION OF THE
DEFENDANT.

95. Now, try reading this. *he kd n fll t — pn wd sbd.*

— — — — — — — — — — — — — — — — —

HE COULD NOT FORETELL THAT THE PAIN WOULD SUBSIDE.

96. Now, can you read this? *s, — kr z @ u svs.*

— — — — — — — — — — — — — — — — —

SIR, THE CAR IS AT YOUR SERVICE.

97. What does this sentence say? *ι h 2 opn a cla @ mlr. Co., Inc. .*

- - - - - - - - - - - - - - - - -

I HAVE TO OPEN A CHARGE ACCOUNT AT MILLER COMPANY, INC.

98. If you want to review, go back to frame 89 to read the QUICKHAND Shorthand again. Otherwise, try your hand at writing some QUICK-HAND sentences.

First, write I BELIEVE THAT HE IS NOT WITH IT.

- - - - - - - - - - - - - - - -

ι blv l he z n w l.

99. Now, write HE WILL RECEIVE HIS REPLY BY OCTOBER 9.

- - - - - - - - - - - - - - -

he l rcv hz rple b Ocl 9.

100. Write PLEASE TELL OUR CHAIRMAN WHICH BOOK YOU PLAN TO RESERVE AT THE LIBRARY.

- - - - - - - - - - - - - - - -

plz ll r crm wc bk u pln 2 rzv @ – lbrr.

101. Now, write THE COMMANDER PAID THE BILL AT THE STORE.

- - - - - - - - - - - - - - -

– kmdr pd – bl @ – str.

102. Now, write HIS FORMER WIFE WOULD NOT PERMIT HIM TO SEE HIS SON.

- - - - - - - - - - - - - - - -

hz fmr wf wd n pml hm 2 c hz sn.

103. Now, write THE JUDGE RULED ON THE MENTAL CONDITION OF THE DEFENDANT.

- - - - - - - - - - - - -

— jj rl n — mll kdy v — dfndnt.

104. Write HE COULD NOT FORETELL THAT THE PAIN WOULD SUBSIDE.

- - - - - - - - - - - - -

he kd n fll l — pn wd ssd.

105. Now, write SIR, THE CAR IS AT YOUR SERVICE.

- - - - - - - - - - - - -

s, — kr z @ u svs.

106. Now, write I HAVE TO OPEN A CHARGE ACCOUNT AT MILLER COMPANY, INC.

- - - - - - - - - - - - -

l h 2 opn a cla @ Mlr. Co., Inc. .

4 chplr 5, u l nd a shrthnd pd. s kkldz chplr 4.

The QUICKHAND above reads: FOR CHAPTER 5, YOU WILL NEED A SHORTHAND PAD. THIS CONCLUDES CHAPTER 4.

go n now 2 — slf - tst 4 s chplr.

The QUICKHAND sentence above says: GO ON NOW TO THE SELF-TEST FOR THIS CHAPTER.

SELF-TEST

A. Write the following words in QUICKHAND

    (1) FORMER _____   (4) WITH _____

    (2) FOREMAN _____   (5) COUNTERACT _____

    (3) PROPER _____   (6) AT _____

B. Transcribe the following words.

    (1) *my* _____   (4) *svs* _____

    (2) *pfx* _____   (5) *wc* _____

    (3) *kdk* _____

C. Write the following sentences in QUICKHAND.

    (1) SIR, THE CAR IS AT YOUR SERVICE.

    ———————————————————————

    (2) I BELIEVE HE IS NOT WITH IT.

    ———————————————————————

D. Transcribe the following sentences.

    (1) *i h 2 opn a cla @ Mhr. Co., Inc..*

    ———————————————————————

    (2) *— jj rl n — mll kdy r — dfndnl.*

    ———————————————————————

E. Write the following sentences (which you have not had before).

    (1) THE SERVICE AT THE PARTY WAS GOOD.

    ———————————————————————

    (2) WE ARE NOT MEMBERS OF THE CONVENTION.

    ———————————————————————

F. Transcribe the following sentences (which you have not had).

    (1) *wc l r — bks dd u lk bsl?*

    ———————————————————————

(2) *he dd n ll me 2 wc aknt he wd chrg — pchs.*

Answers

A. (1) *fmr* ; (2) *fm* ; (3) *ppr* ; (4) *u* ; (5) *kak* ;
   (6) *@*

B. (1) MENTION (or MOTION); (2) PREFIX; (3) CONTRADICT;
   (4) SERVICE; (5) WHICH

C. (1) *s, — kr z @ u svs.*
   (2) *i blv he z n w l.*

D. (1) I HAVE TO OPEN A CHARGE ACCOUNT AT MILLER
       COMPANY, INCORPORATED.
   (2) THE JUDGE RULED ON THE MENTAL CONDITION OF THE
       DEFENDANT.

E. (1) *— svs @ — prl wz gd.*
   (2) *w r n mbrz n — kvny.*

F. (1) WHICH ONE OF THE BOOKS DID YOU LIKE BEST?

   (2) HE DID NOT TELL ME TO WHICH ACCOUNT HE WOULD
       CHARGE THE PURCHASE.

If you would like additional practice before you start the next chapter, turn to the Supplemental Exercise for this chapter in the back of the book.

Chapter Five

1. For this lesson, you will need a shorthand pad. You have already covered all of the word beginnings and endings. If you are not sure of some of them, do not be too concerned. You will have a chance to review them in this chapter.

    In this chapter, you will cover openings and closings of letters, frequently used sounds that occur within words, and one more group of brief forms.

    A great deal of the material that you will be writing in the QUICK-HAND Shorthand System will be business letters. A letter has a salutation and a complimentary close.

    A salutation is the opening of a letter. Examples are: GENTLE-MEN, DEAR SIR, TO WHOM IT MAY CONCERN, DEAR JOHN.

    A complimentary close is the closing of a letter. Examples are: YOURS TRULY, SINCERELY YOURS, LOVE.

    Do you recognize this salutation? *ds*

    _____

    - - - - - - - - - - - - - - -

    DEAR SIR

2. How about this one? *g* _____

    - - - - - - - - - - - - - - -

    GENTLEMEN

3. Do you recognize this? *dmr* _____

    - - - - - - - - - - - - - - -

    DEAR MISTER

4. Use the following abbreviations to indicate the salutations DEAR
    MRS. and DEAR MS.

    DEAR MRS.: *dmrs*   DEAR MS.: *dms*

    Now, see how well you do on complimentary closes. What do you

    think this is? *su* _____

    - - - - - - - - - - - - - -

    SINCERELY YOURS

5. How about this? *vou* _____

    - - - - - - - - - - - - - -

    VERY SINCERELY YOURS

6. What is this? *ru* _____

    - - - - - - - - - - - - - -

    RESPECTFULLY YOURS

7. What is this? *ul* _____

    - - - - - - - - - - - - - -

    YOURS TRULY

8. What is this? *uvl* _____

    - - - - - - - - - - - - - -

    YOURS VERY TRULY

9. How about this? *vlu* _____

    - - - - - - - - - - - - - -

    VERY TRULY YOURS

10. What is *ur* ? _____

    - - - - - - - - - - - - - -

    YOURS RESPECTFULLY

11. What is this? *cu* _____

- - - - - - - - - - - - - -

CORDIALLY YOURS

12. To review, write these salutations: DEAR SIR, DEAR MR.

_____

- - - - - - - - - - - - -

ds , dmr

13. Now, write these complimentary closes: SINCERELY YOURS,
YOURS SINCERELY, YOURS VERY TRULY, VERY TRULY YOURS,
RESPECTFULLY YOURS, YOURS TRULY, CORDIALLY YOURS,
YOURS VERY CORDIALLY.

_____

_____

- - - - - - - - - - - - - -

SINCERELY YOURS: *su*   YOURS SINCERELY: *us*
YOURS VERY TRULY: *uvt*   VERY TRULY YOURS: *vtu*
RESPECTFULLY YOURS: *ru*   YOURS TRULY: *ut*
CORDIALLY YOURS: *cu*   YOURS VERY CORDIALLY: *uvc*

14. Now, you will study frequently used sounds which occur within words.
Many words have NK in them. Some of these NK words are BANK,
RANK, TANK, SANK, LINK, and THINK. NK often comes at the end
of the word, but many words have NK within them. Some of these
words are BANKER, TANKER, LANKY, and THINKING.
      Can you read these NK words and tell how the NK is written?

bk   lk   nk

_____

- - - - - - - - - - - - -

The NK is written *k* . The words in the last frame are BANK,
TANK, and INK.

15. Now you will have an opportunity to write some NK words.

      Write the word RINK. _____

- - - - - - - - - - - - -

rk

16. Write PLANK.   _____

- - - - - - - - - - - - - -

plk

17. Write BANKING.   _____

- - - - - - - - - - - - - -

bk.

18. There are also many English words with ND in them. Some of these words are BAND, HAND, COMMAND, and LAND.

    Can you read these ND words and tell how ND is written?

rmd   kmd   sd

_____

- - - - - - - - - - - - - -

REMAND or REMIND, COMMAND, and SAND or SEND.   You write ND   *d*   .

19. Now, you will have a chance to write some ND words.

    Write LANDING.   _____

- - - - - - - - - - - - - -

ld.

20. Write BANDAGE.   _____

- - - - - - - - - - - - - -

bdj

21. Write DEMAND.   _____

- - - - - - - - - - - - - -

dmd

22. The NT sound also occurs in many words. Some of these words are BENT, DENT, RENT, and SENT.

    Can you read these NT words and tell how NT is written?

    ml   rl   rzl

    _____

    - - - - - - - - - - - - - - -

    MEANT, MINT (or MET, MIT, MAT, MUT), RENT, and RESENT. NT is written *l* .

23. Now, you will have a chance to write some NT words.

    Write TENT. _____

    - - - - - - - - - - - - - - -

    ll

24. Write REPRESENT. _____

    - - - - - - - - - - - - - - -

    rprzl

25. Now, write BENT. _____

    - - - - - - - - - - - - - - -

    bl

26. Now, write VENTILATION. _____

    - - - - - - - - - - - - - - -

    vllg

27. The English language has many words with RD in them. Some of these words are: CARD, HARD, and LARD. Can you read the RD words below and tell how the RD sound is written in QUICKHAND?

    kd   bd

    _____

    - - - - - - - - - - - - - - -

    CARD or CORD and BOARD or BARD. The RD is written *d* .

28. Write the word HARD. _____

- - - - - - - - - - - - - - -

hd

29. Write CARDBOARD. _____

- - - - - - - - - - - - -

kdbd

30. There are also many RK words in English. Some of these words are BARK, HARK, and PARK. Can you read these RK words and tell how to write RK?

ek   mk   rmk   dbk

_____

- - - - - - - - - - - - - -

LARK, MARK, REMARK, and DEBARK. RK is written *k* .

31. Write the word PARKING. _____

- - - - - - - - - - - - - -

pk.

32. Write WORKER. _____

- - - - - - - - - - - - - -

wkr

33. Write MARKET. _____

- - - - - - - - - - - - - -

mkl

34. There are also many RT words in English. Some of these words are MART, HEART, and WART. Can you read these RT words and tell how to write RT?

kl   rpl

_____

- - - - - - - - - - - - - -

CART or COURT and REPORT.   RT is written *ᘰ* .

35. Write QUARTER.   _____

- - - - - - - - - - - - - - -

klr

36. Write PORTER.   _____

- - - - - - - - - - - - -

plr

37. You may have discovered that many English words have TH in them. Some of these words are THESE, THOSE, FATHER, and BROTHER. Can you read the TH words below and tell how the TH is written?

—ru   *—rl*

_____

THROUGH and THRILL.   TH is written with a dash, just like the word THE: *—* .

38. What is this word? *—o*   _____

- - - - - - - - - - - - - -

THOUGH

39. Write THROW.   _____

- - - - - - - - - - - - - -

—ro

40. Write THROUGH.   _____

- - - - - - - - - - - - - -

—ru

41. Write MOTHER.   _____

- - - - - - - - - - - - - - -

m—r

42. Write OTHER. _____

- - - - - - - - - - - - - - -

o—u

43. Write NEITHER. _____

- - - - - - - - - - - - - - -

n—u

44. Can you write THEREFORE? _____

- - - - - - - - - - - - - - -

—rf

45. The CH sound also occurs frequently in English. Some CH words are CHURCH, CHILD, and MUCH. Can you read these CH words and tell how the CH is written?

sc   lc   rc

_____

- - - - - - - - - - - - - - -

The CH is written *c* . The words are SUCH or SEARCH, TOUCH or TEACH, and REACH or ROACH.

46. Write CHILDREN. _____

- - - - - - - - - - - - - - -

cldrn

47. Write PEACH. _____

- - - - - - - - - - - - - - -

pc

48. English also has many SH words. Some of these words are SHIRT, SHIP, and SHOCK. Can you read these words and tell how the SH sound is written?

ʒlhd   ʒp

_____

- - - - - - - - - - - - - - -

SHORTHAND and SHIP (or SHOP). The SH is written *3* .

49. Write SHIPMENT. _____

- - - - - - - - - - - - - - -

3pm

50. Write SHRINK. _____

- - - - - - - - - - - - - - -

3rk

51. The ST blend also occurs frequently in English. Some ST words are START, STOP, and AGAINST. Can you read these ST words and tell how ST is written?

St   Stn

_____

- - - - - - - - - - - - - - -

STEAL, STEEL, STOLE, or STILL, and STOLEN. ST is written with capital *S* .

52. Write RESIST. _____

- - - - - - - - - - - - - - -

rzS

53. Write RESISTANCE. _____

- - - - - - - - - - - - - - -

rzSns

54. Write STING. _____

- - - - - - - - - - - - - - -

S.

55. Another popular blend in English is the OI sound as in BOY, COY, and TOY. Can you read these OI sounding words and tell how the OI sound is written?

jo   ano   dplo

_____

- - - - - - - - - - - - - - - - - -

JOY, ANNOY, and DEPLOY. OI is written *o* .

56. Now, write JOYFUL. _____

- - - - - - - - - - - - - - - - - -

jof

57. Write APPOINT. _____

- - - - - - - - - - - - - - - - - -

apol

58. Now, write APPOINTMENT. _____

- - - - - - - - - - - - - - - - - -

apolm

59. Read the OW words below. See if you can tell how OW is written.

hw   nw   brwn   kw

_____

- - - - - - - - - - - - - - - - - -

HOW NOW BROWN COW. The OW is written *w* .

60. Write COUNT. _____

- - - - - - - - - - - - - - - - - -

kwl

61. Write DOUBT. _____

- - - - - - - - - - - - - - - - - -

dwl

62. The last sound to be covered is the AU sound. This sound occurs in many words. Some of these words are: BOUGHT, CAUGHT, and AWFUL. Can you read the AU words and tell how the AU is written?

sal kal lal

_____

- - - - - - - - - - - - - - -

SOUGHT, CAUGHT, and TAUGHT. The AU sound is written *a* .

63. Write NAUGHT. _____

- - - - - - - - - - - - - - -

nal

64. Write AWFUL. _____

- - - - - - - - - - - - - - -

af

65. You have just covered the last special sound of the course. Before concluding the theory with six more brief forms, let's review what has just been covered by reading and writing some words in QUICK-HAND. If you wish to review special sounds within words first, you may turn back to frame 14 before moving ahead.

What can this word be? *bk* _____

- - - - - - - - - - - - - - -

BANK, BARK, or BOOK

66. Now, write RANK. _____

- - - - - - - - - - - - - - -

rk

67. Write SAND. _____

- - - - - - - - - - - - - - -

sd

68. Write RENT. _____

- - - - - - - - - - - - - - -

rl

69. What can this word be? *dl* _____

- - - - - - - - - - - - - -

DART or DENT

70. Write CARD. _____

- - - - - - - - - - - - - -

kd

71. Write BARK. _____

- - - - - - - - - - - - - -

bk

72. Write MART. _____

- - - - - - - - - - - - - -

ml

73. What can this word be? *ru* _____

- - - - - - - - - - - - - -

THREW or THROUGH

74. Write THOUGHT. _____

- - - - - - - - - - - - - -

al

75. What is this word? *or* _____

- - - - - - - - - - - - - -

OTHER

76. Now, write FATHER. _____

- - - - - - - - - - - - - -

fr

77. What is this word? *sc* _____

- - - - - - - - - - - - - -

SUCH or SEARCH

78. Now, write CHURCH. _____

- - - - - - - - - - - - -

cc

79. What is this word? *3p* _____

- - - - - - - - - - - - - -

SHIP or SHOP

80. Now, write SHOCK. _____

- - - - - - - - - - - - -

3k

81. What is this word? *Sp* _____

- - - - - - - - - - - - -

STOP or STEP

82. Now, write STOVE. _____

- - - - - - - - - - - - -

Sv

83. What is this word? *bo* _____

- - - - - - - - - - - - -

BOY

84. Now, write TOY. _____

- - - - - - - - - - - - -

to

85. What is this word? *hw* _____

- - - - - - - - - - - - - -

HOW

86. Now, write COW. _____

- - - - - - - - - - - - - -

kw

87. What is this word? *ar* _____

- - - - - - - - - - - - - -

AUTHOR

88. Now, write BOUGHT. _____

- - - - - - - - - - - - - -

bal

　　If you want to review the exercises using these special sounds, turn back to frame 65. If you want to review the sounds, turn back to frame 14.

89. Now, you are ready to cover the last six brief forms, making thirty-five you will have had in all. These thirty-five brief forms make up more than forty percent of all the words written in office correspondence.

　　The first brief form in this lesson, number thirty, is FROM. It is written with two letters.

　　How do you think you write FROM? _____

- - - - - - - - - - - - - -

FROM is written *fm* .

90. Word number thirty-one is OR. It is written the same way as ARE.

　　Do you know how to write OR? _____

- - - - - - - - - - - - - -

OR is written *n* .

91. Word thirty-two is AN. Can you guess how to write it?

_____

- - - - - - - - - - - - - - -

AN is written $\mathcal{n}$.

92. The next word, number thirty-three, is WAS. Do you know how to write WAS? _____

- - - - - - - - - - - - - -

WAS is written wz .

93. The next brief form, number thirty-four, is US. Do you know how to write US? _____

- - - - - - - - - - - - - -

US is written $\mathcal{u}$.

94. The last brief form, number thirty-five, is HAS. Do you know how to write HAS? _____

- - - - - - - - - - - - - -

HAS is written $\mathcal{h}$.

If you want to review the brief forms before having a chance to write them, turn back to frame 89.

95. You will now have a chance to write the last six brief forms.

First, write FROM. _____

- - - - - - - - - - - - - -

$\mathcal{fm}$

96. Now, write OR. _____

- - - - - - - - - - - - - -

$\mathcal{n}$

97. Now, write AN. _____

- - - - - - - - - - - - - -

n

98. Now, write WAS. _____

- - - - - - - - - - - - - - -

wz

99. Now, write US. _____

- - - - - - - - - - - - - -

s

100. Now, write HAS. _____

- - - - - - - - - - - - - -

h

If you want to review writing the brief forms in this lesson, go back to frame 95. Otherwise, move ahead to the next frame.

101. You will now have a chance to read a letter in QUICKHAND. Do the best you can. If you miss a few words, don't worry. When you have done your best, look at the English in the answer. Write this letter on your shorthand pad.

dmr Jnz: plz sd s fm u kllg n rdr r #117 pnslz & l - #171 bl pol pnz u kn mk aval. ul,

- - - - - - - - - - - - - - -

Dear Mr. Jones:
Please send us from your catalog an order of number 117 pencils and all the number // 171 ball point pens you can make available.
                                                    Yours truly,

If you have somebody who can dictate and you want to try taking the dictation, have him read the letter to you. There are 34 words in the letter. There are slash marks after the first 20 words. In standard shorthand dictation, 28 syllables count as 20 words. To read at 40 words per minute, the dictator should reach the slashes after 30 seconds and complete the letter in 43 seconds. To read at 50 words per minute, he or she should reach the slashes after 24 seconds and complete the letter after 35 seconds.

102. Now, read the letter below and write the English on your shorthand pad.

[shorthand text]

- - - - - - - - - - - - - - - - -

Dear Mr. Simms:
Thank you for the card you sent us. It has helped to lift our spirits during these dark days.

Sincerely, //

That letter has 20 words. If you have somebody dictate at 40 words per minute, he or she should reach the slash marks (20 words) and complete the letter in 30 seconds. At 50 words per minute, he or she should reach the slashes and complete the letter in 24 seconds.

103. Try reading this and write the English on your shorthand pad.

[shorthand text]

- - - - - - - - - - - - - - - -

Dear Ms. Jackson:
How many times must we ask you to remit the balance on your account for the toys you bought? Your // check must reach us by next Tuesday or we will have to send the account to our attorney.

Respectfully yours,

That letter has 39 words. To read at 40 words per minute, the dictator should reach the slash marks in 30 seconds, and the end of the letter in 59 seconds. To read at 50 words per minute, the dictator should reach the slashes in 24 seconds, and the end of the letter in 47 seconds.

104. You will now be given another letter. Write it the best you can in QUICKHAND and then check your work against the QUICKHAND Shorthand in the answer. Don't worry if your QUICKHAND is different from that in the book. The most important part of QUICKHAND is to be able to read back what you write.

This letter will have 27 words. There are slashes after the first 20 words. If you have somebody dictate and he or she reads at 40 words per minute, he or she should reach the slashes in 30 seconds and the end of the letter in 41 seconds. At 50 words per minute, the reader should reach the slashes in 24 seconds and the end of the letter in 32 seconds.

Try writing this letter in QUICKHAND on your shorthand pad.

Dear Ms:
We can wait no longer for the information we requested in our letter of more than two weeks ago. // Please reply promptly.

Yours truly,

- - - - - - - - - - - - - - - - -

How did you do? If it went slowly, you may try again. Otherwise, try reading the letter back from your own notes. This is the most important part of QUICKHAND. Our QUICKHAND is shown below.

Again, don't be too concerned if some of your QUICKHAND words are written differently from the way they are in the book. If you can read back your own notes, even with a struggle at first, you are doing all right. If you want to, you may try the letter again now that you have seen it in the QUICKHAND Shorthand.

105. The last letter is a long letter. If you are not sure of a word, put down something and continue writing the rest of the letter. If you write something, even though it may not be correct, you may well be able to read it back anyway. If you stop to try to write it correctly, you are likely to miss the rest of the sentence or even the rest of the letter. If somebody is dictating to you, he or she should use the chart below to determine when to reach the slash marks for various speeds of dictation.

Speed	First	Second	Complete
40 wpm	30 seconds	60 seconds	68 seconds
45 wpm	27 seconds	54 seconds	60 seconds
50 wpm	24 seconds	48 seconds	54 seconds
55 wpm	22 seconds	44 seconds	50 seconds
60 wpm	20 seconds	40 seconds	45 seconds

Dear Mr. Mack:
We wish to thank you for the purchases you have made at our store. We would like to inform you that // you may shop at any of our other stores should they be more convenient. There are eleven stores in our chain to // serve you.

Very truly yours,

- - - - - - - - - - - - - - - - -

How did it go? If you had a struggle, go back and try again. If you did well and you have somebody to dictate, you may want to try again at a higher speed. Our QUICKHAND is shown below.

dmr mk: w wz 2 —k u 4 —pcs u h md @ r Sr. w wd lk 2 nfm u l u ma zp @ ne v r o r Srz zd —a b mr kvnl. —r r || Srz nr cn 2 sv u. vlu,

If you wish, you may try the letter again now that you have seen it in QUICKHAND. Otherwise, you have completed the theory part of your course. It is only a matter of practice until you take dictation at eighty words per minute or faster. Dictation from actual letters or from any good dictation book will help you achieve this goal quickly. Dictation will give you an opportunity to practice the principles and brief forms you have learned in this course. In the back of this book, you will find a glossary of brief forms and special sounds. You may want to review the glossary before you start any dictation. Of course, it is there for reference at any time you need it.

But go on now to the Self-Test for this chapter, to see how well you have grasped its content.

SELF-TEST

A. Write the following words in QUICKHAND.

(1) BOOK _____   (6) CORK _____

(2) SAND _____   (7) DARK _____

(3) SENT _____   (8) CHURCH _____

(4) CARD _____   (9) SHOP _____

(5) DART _____   (10) STOP _____

B. Transcribe the following words.

(1) *Sl* _____   (6) *kal* _____

(2) *lo* _____   (7) *fm* _____

(3) *nw* _____   (8) *k* _____

(4) *hw* _____   (9) *s* _____

(5) *bal* _____   (10) *kn* _____

C. Write the following letter (which you have not had before) in QUICK-
HAND. Use your shorthand pad.

Gentlemen:
We have on hand some very pretty cups with gold bands around the
top. We wonder if you could use them at a special price to close
them out.

Yours very truly,

D. Transcribe the following.

dmr mk: w wz 2 k u 4- pcs u h md @ r Sr. w wd lk 2 nfm u t u ma gp @ ne vr r or Srz gd a b mr kvnl. r r ‖ Srz n r en 2 sv u. vlu,

E. Write the following (which you have not had) in QUICKHAND.

Dear Sir:
Your good order came early today. We will make every effort to
ship it tomorrow just as you requested.

Sincerely,

F. Transcribe the following.

j: - bdz w h r 5' wd + 4' hu. r r onl 2 pr lf. ma w zp -m 2 u? ul,

Answers

A. (1) *bk* ; (2) *ad* ; (3) *ol* ; (4) *kd* ; (5) *dl* ; (6) *kk* ;
(7) *dk* ; (8) *cc* ; (9) *zp* ; (10) *Sp*

B. (1) START (or STREET); (2) TOY; (3) NOW; (4) HOW; (5) BOUGHT;
(6) CAUGHT; (7) FROM; (8) HAS; (9) US (or THIS); (10) CAN

C. *j: w h n hd sm vr prl kps w gld bdz arwd -lp. w wdr f u kd uz -m @ a spj prs 2 klz -m wt. uvt,*

D. Dear Mr. Mack:
We wish to thank you for the purchases you have made at our store.
We would like to inform you that you may shop at any of our other
stores should they be more convenient. There are eleven stores in
our chain to serve you.

Very truly yours,

E. *ds: u gd rdr km rl 2da. w l mk evr ft 2 zp l 2mro js z u rks. s,*

F.   Gentlemen:
     The beds we have are five feet wide and four feet high.   There are
     only two pair left.   May we ship them to you?

                                                        Yours truly,

     If you would like additional practice, turn now to the Supplemental
Exercise for this final chapter.

Supplemental Exercises

CHAPTER 2

Here are some additional exercises for Chapter 2. Sentences in section A are relatively short and simple. The ones in B are more difficult.

Have someone dictate the English sentences while you write them in QUICKHAND. Then transcribe the QUICKHAND back into English and check the answers. Or. if no one is available for dictation, transcribe the QUICKHAND sentences below into English. (If you have difficulty, check the English answers and then try the transcription again.)

A.   Transcribe the following sentences.

(1) *ak sn. u ma m — spr sl.*

(2) *i l b ab 2 k o @ 4:00.*

(3) *plz mk a pam z sn z u kn.*

(4) *brn lf @ — ups.*

(5) *he z — hd v — ofs.*

(6) *w hp 2 c u agn sn.*

(7) *kpr & klrsl — 2 bks.*

(8) *— kr ndz n ohl.*

(9) *u dumt sm 2 ustd — kprsn.*

(10) *du u hv a spx pln ?*

The sentences are:

(1) ACT SOON. YOU MAY MISS THE SPECIAL SALE.
(2) I WILL BE ABLE TO COME OVER AT 4:00.
(3) PLEASE MAKE A PAYMENT AS SOON AS YOU CAN.
(4) TURN LEFT AT THE UNDERPASS.
(5) HE IS THE HEAD OF THE OFFICE.
(6) WE HOPE TO SEE YOU AGAIN SOON.
(7) COMPARE AND CONTRAST THE TWO BOOKS.
(8) THE CAR NEEDS AN OVERHAUL.
(9) YOU DO NOT SEEM TO UNDERSTAND THE COMPARISON.
(10) DO YOU HAVE A SPECIAL PLAN?

B. (1) *u ma wnt 2 dks — pblm v u bl @ — mgr's ofs.*

(2) *u ma b ab 2 km 2 — dky aftr — mt. @ 6:00.*

(3) *u du nt ustd — aky u r dks.*

(4) *du nt mk a mtk wn u ppr — ktrk.*

(5) *wl u b ab 2 ktk hr 4 — mt. ?*

(6) *w wl hv — dky 2 kpr — 2 plnz.*

(7) *trn rt wn u gt 2 — ups & u wl b n rt. 18.*

(8) *wl u 9 — mbrz ∾ u kls b ab 2 k o 4 — prl ?*

(9) *i md —mlk ∾ kl. 4 — ml. bfr — wknd.*

(10) *he wz grx 2 h — ml. @ hz hs.*

The sentences are:

(1) YOU MAY WANT TO DISCUSS THE PROBLEM OF YOUR BILL AT THE MANAGER'S OFFICE.
(2) I MAY BE ABLE TO COME TO THE DISCUSSION AFTER THE MEETING AT 6:00.
(3) I DO NOT UNDERSTAND THE ACTION YOU ARE DISCUSSING.
(4) DO NOT MAKE A MISTAKE WHEN YOU PREPARE THE CON-TRACT.
(5) WILL YOU BE ABLE TO CONTACT HER FOR THE MEETING?
(6) WE WILL HAVE THE DISCUSSION TO COMPARE THE TWO PLANS.
(7) TURN RIGHT WHEN YOU GET TO THE UNDERPASS AND YOU WILL BE ON ROUTE 18.
(8) WILL YOU AND THE MEMBERS OF YOUR CLASS BE ABLE TO COME OVER FOR THE PARTY?
(9) I MADE THE MISTAKE OF CALLING FOR THE MEETING BE-FORE THE WEEKEND.
(10) HE WAS GRACIOUS TO HAVE THE MEETING AT HIS HOUSE.

CHAPTER 3

Here are some additional exercises for Chapter 3. The sentences in sec-tion A are relatively short and simple. The ones in B are more difficult.

Have someone dictate the English sentences while you write them in QUICKHAND. Then transcribe the QUICKHAND back into English and check the answers. Or, if no one is available for dictation, transcribe the QUICKHAND sentences following into English. (If you have difficulty, check the English answers and then try the transcription again.)

A. Transcribe the following sentences.

(1) *w l h a spkr @ — ml. .*

(2) *du u rkl — kpll adrs ?*

(3) *w l wt ntll he kz.*

(4) *plz du u bst 2 rkl — mtr fl.*

(5) *w r nu n — nbrhd.*

(6) *s z n mpll mtr.*

(7) *w l tk a nmbr v ppl 2 — mt. .*

(8) *du u h tprt ?*

(9) *w l sn b @ — nd v — prd.*

(10) *mk u pam @ — nd v — wk.*

Tne sentences are:

(1) WE WILL HAVE A SPEAKER AT THE MEETING.
(2) DO YOU RECALL THE COMPLETE ADDRESS?
(3) WE WILL WAIT UNTIL HE COMES.
(4) PLEASE DO YOUR BEST TO RECALL THE MATTER FULLY.
(5) WE ARE NEW IN THE NEIGHBORHOOD.
(6) THIS IS AN IMPORTANT MATTER.
(7) WE WILL TAKE A NUMBER OF PEOPLE TO THE MEETING.
(8) DO YOU HAVE TRANSPORTATION?
(9) WE WILL SOON BE AT THE END OF THE PERIOD.
(10) MAKE YOUR PAYMENT AT THE END OF THE WEEK.

B.   (1) *go —ru — cl & trn lf @ — nsky.*

(2) *u du nt aluz rt a kpll sntns.*

(3) *l u b ab 2 tk atndns @ — mtl. n Tue.?*

(4) *w-h hd sm tprty pblmz n — nbrhd.*

(5) *du u fl ustnd — mprtns v — mtr?*

(6) *trn lf ftr — intsk & u l b @ — mn nns.*

The sentences are:

(1) GO THROUGH THE CIRCLE AND TURN LEFT AT THE INTER-
SECTION.
(2) YOU DO NOT ALWAYS WRITE A COMPLETE SENTENCE.
(3) WILL YOU BE ABLE TO TAKE ATTENDANCE AT THE MEET-
ING ON TUESDAY?
(4) WE HAVE HAD SOME TRANSPORTATION PROBLEMS IN THE
NEIGHBORHOOD.
(5) DO YOU FULLY UNDERSTAND THE IMPORTANCE OF THE
MATTER?
(6) TURN LEFT AFTER THE INTERSECTION AND YOU WILL BE
AT THE MAIN ENTRANCE.

CHAPTER 4

Here are some additional exercises for Chapter 4. The sentences in
section A are relatively short and simple. The ones in section B are
more difficult.

Have someone dictate the English sentences while you write them in
QUICKHAND. Then transcribe the QUICKHAND back into English and
check your answers. Or, if no one is available to dictate to you, simply
transcribe the QUICKHAND sentences following into English. (If you are
transcribing on your own and have difficulty, check the English in the
answer section and then try the transcription again.)

A. Transcribe the following sentences.

(1) *msl v — sjks wr msl.*

(2) *i l ml Bl & Mr 4 — prt.*

(3) *wr l mk a kofr 2 — ppzl.*

(4) *he wd n mk ne almp 2 ml hr.*

(5) *s rnz k 2 — oal pln.*

(6) *s ma n b a gd dl 4 — fmrz.*

(7) *wc da z blr 4 — prt?*

(8) *plz b thr @ 3:00.*

(9) *i am sr l i fgt — nm v — skl.*

(10) *i l b krf n 2 b ll 4 — kls.*

The sentences are:

(1) MOST OF THE SUBJECTS WERE INTERESTING.
(2) I WILL MEET BILL AND MARY FOR THE PARTY.
(3) WE WILL MAKE A COUNTEROFFER TO THE PROPOSAL.
(4) HE WOULD NOT MAKE ANY ATTEMPT TO MEET HER.
(5) THIS RUNS COUNTER TO THE OVERALL PLAN.
(6) THIS MAY NOT BE A GOOD DEAL FOR THE FARMERS.
(7) WHICH DAY IS BETTER FOR THE PARTY?
(8) PLEASE BE THERE AT 3:00.
(9) I AM SORRY THAT I FORGOT THE NAME OF THE SCHOOL.
(10) I WILL BE CAREFUL NOT TO BE LATE FOR THE CLASS.

B. (1) *hw fr shld w go fllr w go u - ops ?*

(2) *plz ppr 2 pwd - mbrz w a kpll rpt.*

(3) *- svs @ - dnr wz vr gd.*

(4) *s kdks mc v wt u tk abt rlr.*

(5) *w l mk r dsy @ - ml. n -9 - r -1 n - 16.*

(6) *i l b @ - sy @ 2:00 & @ - 1 @ 3:30.*

The sentences are:

(1) HOW FAR SHOULD WE GO AFTER WE GO UNDER THE OVER-PASS?
(2) PLEASE PREPARE TO PROVIDE THE MEMBERS WITH A COMPLETE REPORT.
(3) THE SERVICE AT THE DINNER WAS VERY GOOD.
(4) THIS CONTRADICTS MUCH OF WHAT YOU TALKED ABOUT EARLIER.
(5) WE WILL MAKE OUR DECISION AT THE MEETING ON THE NINTH OR THE ONE ON THE SIXTEENTH.
(6) I WILL BE AT THE SESSION AT 2:00 AND AT THE ONE AT 3:30.

CHAPTER 5

Here are some additional exercises for Chapter 5. The letters in section A are relatively short and simple. The ones in section B are more difficult.

Have someone dictate the letters while you write them in QUICKHAND. Then transcribe the QUICKHAND back into English and check your letters with the originals. Or, if no one is available to dictate to you, simply transcribe the QUICKHAND letters into English. (If you have difficulty, check the answers and then try to read the QUICKHAND again.)

A.　Transcribe the following letters.

(1)　*d Dk: -r r no gps n - lps. ec lp z rkd fm bgn. 2 nd. w r vr hp w - kwll r r lps. ul,*

_____

_____

_____

_____

(2)　*d Pm: -ks 4 - rdr u gv s lS wk 9 4 l v u rdrz. // bkz r lbr pblmz, w h n bn ab 2 gl splz w nd 9 h a bklg r rdrz 4 me r r pdks. f - lbr pblmz r n slo blwn nw 9 - nd r - mv, w l mpl mlrl fm abrad 9 w zd b ab 2 ml r bklg. su,*

_____

_____

_____

_____

_____

_____

(3)　*d Jk: Mr. C.T. Ryrg r - N.Y. ofs l b n - area 4 - nx 3 r 4 daz. w l vr hp 2 h hm hr. plz du wl u k 2 mk l psb 4 - ppl n u sky 2 h a cnc 2 ml w hm. su,*

_____
_____
_____
_____
_____
_____

The letters are:

(1) Dear Dick:
There are no gaps in the tapes. Each tape is recorded from beginning to end. We are very happy with the quality of our tapes.

Yours truly,

(2) Dear Pam:
Thanks for the order you gave us last week and for all of your orders.

Because of labor problems, we have not been able to get supplies we need and have a backlog of orders for many of our products.

If the labor problems are not solved between now and the end of the month, we will import material from abroad and we should be able to meet our backlog.

Sincerely yours,

(3) Dear Jack:
Mr. C. T. Rogers of the New York office will be in the area for the next three or four days. We are very happy to have him here. Please do what you can to make it possible for the people in your section to have a chance to meet with him.

Sincerely yours,

B. Transcribe the following letters.

(1) [shorthand notation]

(2) d Pal: w wr hp 2 c u q — o r mbrz v
u fml. w hp l u q u cldrn l b ab 2 vzl
s agn sm lm pn. // — nx lm u r n lwn,
w hp — r l b mr lm b— 2 vzl w s q 2 c
sm v — alrkyz n — area. // agn, w wr gld 2
c u fml. ul,

(3) d Im: ks 4 — hlp u gv s n r dkyy rll. 2
— aplky w rsll fil. // r u go. 2 — ml. 4 —
rynl ofsrz n — q— ? // f u r go. 2 — ml,
phps w k gl 2g—r bf l Sls r @ lS bf
w go 2 — dnr. ul,

_____

_____

_____

_____

_____

_____

_____

The letters are:

(1)   Dear Nancy,
      As of the first of the year we are moving to our new location in
      the downtown area of the city.
          We hope that this move will be convenient for you and the
      rest of our customers.
          We hope to see your family and many of your friends in our
      new office soon.

                                                  Sincerely,

(2)   Dear Pat:
      We were happy to see you and the other members of your family.
      We hope that you and your children will be able to visit us again
      some time soon.
          The next time you are in town, we hope there will be more
      time both to visit with us and to see some of the attractions in
      the area.
          Again, we were glad to see your family.

                                                  Yours truly,

(3)   Dear ,Tom (or Tim):
      Thanks for the help you gave us in our discussions relating to
      the application we recently filed.
          Are you going to the meeting for the regional officers on the
      9th?
          If you are going to the meeting, perhaps we can get together
      before it starts or at least before we go to the dinner.

                                                  Yours truly,

Appendix

If you are reading this Appendix, you probably want to learn more about QUICKHAND and traditional shorthand systems.

A great many people have had difficulty with traditional shorthand courses. Perhaps you yourself have had a frustrating experience with some other shorthand system. One writer states, in a recent article, that you have plenty of company.

> Research reports indicate that after completing one year of shorthand instruction in high school, less than twenty percent of the students are capable of taking dictation at sixty words a minute. Even more appalling, the same reports show that after completing two years of shorthand instruction, less than fifty percent of the students are capable of taking dictation at eighty words a minute. (1)

In other words, less than one student in five can write in shorthand at 60 words a minute after a year of class. Practically everybody can write 35 words a minute in English longhand with no instruction whatever. In fact, just by getting used to writing fast and using a few standard abbreviations, most people can probably learn to write close to 60 words a minute without any training at all.

The purpose of this discussion is to give some insight into what shorthand is, how it has developed and how the QUICKHAND system has made use of scientific studies to make this program as easy as possible and to reduce the drop-out rate.

HISTORY AND DEVELOPMENT OF SHORTHAND SYSTEMS

When most people hear the word shorthand, they think of traditional Gregg Shorthand. A few people may think of Pitman Shorthand and some might think of an alphabetic system such as Speedwriting.

Most people probably do not realize that there have been shorthand systems for many centuries. Carvings by cave dwellers and Egyptian hieroglyphics are really forms of shorthand.

In a recent article, Edward L. Christensen traces the history of

(1) Joe M. Pullis, Methods of Shorthand Instruction, A Research Analysis, Monograph #126, Southwestern Publishing Company, Cincinnati, Ohio, 1973.

shorthand from 1588 to the present. (2) He mentions one shorthand system in the 16th century by Bright, four in the 17th century by Willis, Shelton, Coles, and Dix, three in the 18th century by Blanchard, Pocknell, and Byrom, and a great many in the 19th century. Nineteenth century systems include those by Sloan, Stackhouse, Prepian, Deploye, Oxley, and Deployan, as well as those by Gregg and Pitman.

The early symbol shorthand systems can be divided both into light-line systems and shaded systems. Shaded systems, including Pitman, make use of light and dark strokes. A light comma may stand for one letter of the alphabet and a dark comma for a second letter. A light, large comma could be a third letter and a dark, large comma a fourth letter. As a result of using both symbols and shading, such systems take a long time to learn and are very difficult for many students to master.

By far the most frequently used light-line system in English is the Gregg shorthand system. It makes use of various symbols to represent different letters but does not use any shading.

Shorthand systems using letters of the alphabet have become popular fairly recently. Today, many employees who need shorthand only take two or three letters a day once or twice or three times a week. They need to be able to take shorthand, yet they probably spend only a half an hour or forty-five minutes a week taking shorthand and only three or four hours of their work week transcribing it. Learning symbol systems and the new symbol alphabets such as in Gregg shorthand takes two years. For people who use shorthand only as an incidental part of their jobs, this is costly and takes much too long.

In 1882, Thomas Anderson delivered a paper before the British Shorthand Society. In that paper, he made several general criticisms of the shorthand systems of his time. Surprisingly, most of these criticisms still have not been answered.

Anderson believed that a single symbol should represent every letter and that every symbol should be readily joined with another symbol. In Gregg shorthand today, there are two different ways to write the letter S.

Anderson also thought that characters should be written on one slope. This recommendation has not been acted upon in traditional Gregg shorthand. Anderson also thought that rules for abbreviation should be "sure, comprehensive and few." Today there are about 150 brief forms and a great many other abbreviations in traditional shorthand. Practically every shorthand system has at least 100 special abbreviations. The rules for the abbreviations are hardly "sure, comprehensive and few."

The QUICKHAND system answers Anderson's questions. There is only one way to write each letter. All letters join readily with all other letters. All letters are written on one slope.

_____

(2) Edward L. Christensen, "Five Crucial Features of a Shorthand System," The Balance Sheet, Southwestern Publishing Company, Cincinnati, Ohio, 1974, pp. 52—56.

The rules for QUICKHAND abbreviations are "sure, comprehensive and few." Only the most frequently used English words are written with brief forms. Also, only the most frequently used word endings, word beginnings, and two-word phrases are abbreviated. There are no exceptions to the rules for abbreviations.

Today, there are a number of alphabetic shorthand systems. Unfortunately, the major difference between symbol systems and most alphabetic systems is just that the alphabetic systems use letters of the alphabet. Most alphabetic systems incorporate many of the same weak points the traditional symbol systems have.

ADDITIONAL DIFFICULTIES WITH
TRADITIONAL SHORTHAND SYSTEMS

There are several reasons why so many students do not attain proficiency in traditional shorthand. First of all, before a student really begins to write shorthand, he must learn a complete new alphabet, much as he would have to do if he studied Arabic or Chinese. He learns to write the S and the V with various sizes of commas, the O, R, and L with various varieties of curves, the D and the T and the N and the M with various sizes and directions of slants and dashes and most of the vowels with various sizes and varieties of circles. The student must learn the entire shorthand alphabet. This takes a great deal of time. It also takes a well motivated student who is willing to work very hard and who has the capacity to learn the new language.

A second major reason that a great many students have not been successful in learning traditional shorthand is that until QUICKHAND was published in 1974, shorthand systems showed very little relationship to the English language as it is actually used.

For example, 10 words in English make up about one-quarter of all the words ever used. The words THE, OF, TO, AND, IN, YOU, A, WE, FOR, and YOUR comprise about one-quarter of all the words ever used— 24.67 percent in Silverthorn's Study(3), and 25.71 percent in Perry's Study(4). Silverthorn scientifically selected material that totaled 300,000 words. In this material, one word which is a brief form in traditional shorthand, OBJECTED, did not appear at all. Three other special abbreviations (brief forms) appeared only once. If a person takes ten average length letters in shorthand during the average week, he would never come across the word OBJECTED and would have a chance to write the other three words only once every four years.

Of the 151 brief forms in traditional shorthand, according to Silverthorn's list, 82 of them, or more than half, were used less than once

---

(3) James E. Silverthorn, Unpublished Doctoral Dissertation, Indiana University, June 1955.

(4) Devern J. Perry, Unpublished Doctoral Dissertation, University of North Dakota, Grand Forks, North Dakota, August 1968.

every 900 words or less often than twice a week for the stenographer who takes ten letters a week.

By the same token, according to Pullis, 46 of the 100 most used words in English are not brief forms(5).

Therefore, a student must learn many brief forms for words which he hardly ever uses and has no brief forms for some of the most used English words.

No wonder so many people who once studied shorthand have to take refresher courses! Even if they take a few letters a week, there are many words which they won't write more than once a week. How can they be expected to remember them?

The QUICKHAND shorthand system has brief forms for only frequently used words. There are only 35 brief forms and each of them is used at least once every 325 words, or about once every two letters. There is a brief form for all frequently used words and there are no brief forms for words that are not frequently used.

QUICKHAND also has special abbreviations for only the most used word beginnings, word endings, and sounds that occur frequently within words.

Another problem with traditional shorthand is that the practice dictation material is not at all related to the type of material that a student will write on the job. In the early lessons, the student has not had brief forms for the most used words and therefore cannot write meaningful paragraphs until he has had abbreviations for words such as THE, OF, TO, AND, IN, and YOU. High speed dictation in many of the traditional Gregg shorthand books comes from the Congressional Record. While a person who is going to be a Congressional reporter or a secretary to a Congressman might find practicing such material useful, many long and complicated words in this material are hardly ever used in the average office situation.

It seems as if the shorthand letters in most of the shorthand textbooks were not carefully chosen. For example, in one widely used shorthand dictation book, the name of the month AUGUST is used several times as often as it should be, while the names of some of the other months are used only a fraction of the number of times they appear in business communications. Students using that book may know how to write AUGUST, but there is a good chance that they don't know or will soon forget how to write the names of the other months. It looks as if, for this particular book, the author took a file of letters written in August.

QUICKHAND is the only program which, in its practice material, uses each of the eight most frequently used English words in the same rank order as they occur in both Silverthorn's and Perry's studies and the ten most frequently used English words in approximately the same percentages as they occur in these two studies.

---

(5) Pullis, op. cit.

DEVELOPMENT OF QUICKHAND SHORTHAND

We have already discussed briefly three major features of the QUICK-HAND shorthand program which should make it relatively easy for students to learn.

First, QUICKHAND is an alphabetic shorthand system. Students use letters of the alphabet. Second, QUICKHAND brief forms, word beginnings and word endings are based on words, word beginnings, and word endings which occur frequently in English. If material occurs frequently, the student will be able to write it quickly with an abbreviation. He will use abbreviations frequently enough so that he will remember them. If material comes up rarely, it is written the way it sounds.

The third innovation is that the exercises in the practice material have the same proportion of the words that appear frequently in the English language as do office letters. A student will write all of the frequently used words often enough so that he will remember their QUICKHAND abbreviations.

In addition to all of these features, QUICKHAND has incorporated other features as the result of extensive pilot tests among students. Before the book was published, five groups of about twenty students each went through the book and indicated any vocabulary words that they did not understand, any sections of the text that seemed confusing, and any questions for which they did not give the right answers. As a result of the experiences of these students, several important changes were made.

In the pilot testing, it was discovered that many students were not familiar with certain vocabulary words. Many students had trouble learning about prefixes because they did not know what a "prefix" was. As it is not really necessary to know the meaning of the term "prefix" to learn shorthand, the term "word beginning" is used instead. Also, the term "word ending" is used instead of "suffix."

Also, a number of students did not know the meaning of the term "vowel." Because it would be difficult to learn shorthand without knowing this definition, a frame was added to explain this term.

There are several other unique features about the QUICKHAND system. Many educational psychologists believe that when a student is given an opportunity to discover material for himself, he is more likely to remember the material than if he is told a principle or a rule. Therefore, instead of saying MIS is written with an M and DIS is written with a D, QUICKHAND students have a chance to discover these principles for themselves.

QUICKHAND also uses a branching programmed instruction technique. There are optional exercises for students who need extra work, while students who are already familiar with the work can skip ahead.

Another innovation is that students are encouraged to learn frequently used words much the same way they learn frequently used phone numbers—by using them over and over again. Many educational psychologists believe that a student is more likely to learn and remember the shorthand abbreviation for the word THE by using it many times and by reading and writing it in sentences, paragraphs, articles, and letters, than by writing THE fifty times by itself.

The QUICKHAND program, as it is today, reflects an enlightened attitude toward teaching and learning. Until recently, if the student had a difficult time learning a course, many teachers, authors, and publishers would think that there was something wrong with the student. If a lot of students failed shorthand, people would say, "Well, I guess they're just not bright enough and they don't work hard enough to learn shorthand."

EVALUATION

The QUICKHAND philosophy is that if a great many students have difficulty learning, the instruction and the text should be changed so that fewer students have difficulty. If a student fails or drops out of a course before reaching his objective, it does not necessarily mean that there is anything wrong with the student.

We constantly contact teachers and students who have studied QUICKHAND and ask them for their experiences and what changes they would make if they had a chance to write a new edition of the book. We believe that such suggestions will help us in further improving our course. We would appreciate your comments, submitted on the evaluation form on the following page.

Please complete this information as fully as possible. If you need more room, write on the other side of the page or attach an additional page.

1. What was your objective in taking this course?

2. Do you believe that you met this objective?

3. What vocabulary words, if any, did you not understand or find difficult to understand?

4. What sections of the course, if any, did you find difficult to understand?

5. Did you enjoy the course?

6. Which sections of the course were most enjoyable?

7. Were there any parts of the course that you did not particularly enjoy? Which sections of the course were these?

8. If you had a chance to prepare a revised edition of this course, what changes would you make?

9. Other Comments:
    Last school grade completed _____ Studied shorthand before? _____

    If yes, what shorthand system? _____ For how long? _____

Optional

Name _____

Address _____ Telephone _____

City _____ State _____ Zip _____

We sincerely appreciate your evaluation of the course. All student and faculty evaluations will be seriously considered before we publish a new edition.

Send your evaluation form to:

Editor, Self-Teaching Guides
John Wiley & Sons, Inc.
605 Third Avenue
New York, New York 10016

Final Self-Test

The minimum passing score is no more than twenty errors. Each word that is written incorrectly in either QUICKHAND or English counts as one error. For example, if two words in shorthand in number 5 are not the same as they are in the answer key, it counts as two errors. You have passed the test if you have twenty errors or less.

1. Write the following words in QUICKHAND.

   (1) HAVE _____   (9) FROM _____

   (2) OUR _____   (10) THIS _____

   (3) WHICH _____   (11) WAS _____

   (4) WOULD _____   (12) AS _____

   (5) YOUR _____   (13) HAS _____

   (6) IF _____   (14) AND _____

   (7) NOT _____   (15) BY _____

   (8) FOR _____

2. Write the following words in English.

   (1) _a_ _____   (11) _l_ _____

   (2) _ᴎ_ _____   (12) _ᴎ_ _____

   (3) _—_ _____   (13) _m_ _____

   (4) _ꜱ_ _____   (14) _w_ _____

   (5) _ι_ _____   (15) _ʒ_ _____

   (6) _2_ _____   (16) _ℒ_ _____

   (7) _ᴫ_ _____   (17) _ℓ_ _____

   (8) _m_ _____   (18) _w_ _____

   (9) _@_ _____   (19) _m_ _____

   (10) _l_ _____   (20) _u_ _____

3. Write the following in English. Use your shorthand pad.

[shorthand text]

4. Write the following in English.

[shorthand text]

5. On a separate sheet of paper, write the following in QUICKHAND.

Dear Sam:
Thanks for the advice you gave me.
    We plan to mail the application to the board before the end of the week.
        Please get in touch with us if we can help in any way.
                                                Yours truly,

6. On a separate sheet of paper, write the following in QUICKHAND.

Dear Jack:
Mr. C. T. Rogers of the New York office will be in the area for the next three or four days. We are very happy to have him here. Please do what you can to make it possible for the people in your section to have a chance to meet with him.
                                                Sincerely yours,

For questions 7 and 8, use only your QUICKHAND notes from questions 5 and 6 (on the separate sheets).

7. Look at your response to question 5. Write the letter in English.

8. Look at your response to question 6. Write the letter in English.

Answers

1. (1)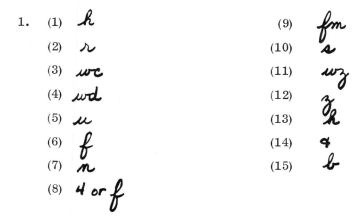

    (2)

    (3)

    (4)

    (5)

    (6)

    (7)

    (8)

    (9)

    (10)

    (11)

    (12)

    (13)

    (14)

    (15)

2. If there is more than one word in the answer, you are correct if you write any one of those words.

    (1) A
    (2) OF
    (3) THE
    (4) THIS
    (5) I
    (6) TO
    (7) ARE, OR, OUR
    (8) IN, ON, AN
    (9) AT
    (10) THAT, IT

    (11) THAT, IT
    (12) OR, ARE, OUR
    (13) IN, AN, ON
    (14) WITH, WE
    (15) AS, IS
    (16) BY, BE
    (17) WILL
    (18) WE, WITH
    (19) NOT
    (20) YOUR, YOU

3. Dear Dick,
    There are no gaps in the tapes. Each tape is recorded from beginning to end. We are happy with the quality of the tapes.

    Yours truly,

4. Dear Nancy,
    As of the first of the year we are moving to our new location in the downtown area of the city.
    We hope that this move will be convenient for you and the rest of our customers.
    We hope to see your family and many of your friends in our new office soon.

    Sincerely,

5. *[shorthand]* d Sm: ks 4 — adrs u gv me. // w pln 2
ml — aplky 2 — bd bf — md v — wk. // plz
gl n lc w s f w ken hlp n ne wa. ul,

6. *[shorthand]* d Jk: Mr. C.T. Ryrz v — n.y. ofs l b n — area
4 — mx 3 r 4 daz. w r vr hp 2 h hm hr.
plz du wat u ken 2 mk l psb 4 — ppl n
u sky 2 h a cns 2 ml w hm. su,

Answers for 7 and 8 in questions 5 and 6 above.

Glossary

1.	a	*a*	25.	this	*ᵴ*	
2.	an	*n*	26.	to	*2*	
3.	and	*+*	27.	us	*ᵴ*	
4.	are	*r*	28.	was	*wz*	
5.	as	*ȝ*	29.	we	*w*	
6.	at	*@*	30.	which	*wc*	
7.	be	*b*	31.	will	*l*	
8.	by	*b*	32.	with	*w*	
9.	for	*4 or f*	33.	would	*wd*	
10.	from	*fm*	34.	you	*u*	
11.	has	*h*	35.	your	*u*	
12.	have	*h*				
13.	I	*ι*	WORD BEGINNINGS			
14.	if	*f*	1.	circ, circum, circu	*c*	
15.	in	*n*	2.	com, con, contra	*k*	
16.	is	*ȝ*	3.	dis	*d*	
17.	it	*ι*	4.	enter, inter	*n*	
18.	not	*n*	5.	far, fir, fur, ful, for	*f*	
19.	of	*v*	6.	men, min, mon, man	*m*	
20.	on	*n*	7.	mis	*m*	
21.	or	*r*	8.	over	*o*	
22.	our	*r*	9.	pre, pro, pur	*p*	
23.	that	*l*	10.	re	*r*	
24.	the	*—*	11.	ser	*ᵴ*	

125

12.	sub	*s*
13.	trans	*l*
14.	un, under	*u*

WORD ENDINGS

1.	ance, ence	*ns*
2.	ble	*b*
3.	cial, tial, cious, tious	*x*
4.	fill, ful	*f*
5.	hood	*hd*
6.	ing	*·*
7.	ly	*l*
8.	ment	*m*
9.	ry	*r*
10.	tion	*f*
11.	tive	*v*
12.	ward	*wd*

SOUNDS WITHIN WORDS

1.	au	*a*
2.	ch	*c*
3.	nd	*d*
4.	nk	*k*
5.	nt	*l*
6.	oi, oy	*o*
7.	ow	*w*
8.	rd	*d*
9.	rk	*k*
10.	rt	*l*
11.	sh	*z*
12.	st	*s*
13.	th	*—*

Dictionary

a	*a*	an	*n*
able	*ab*	and	*+*
about	*abwl*	annual	*nul*
above	*abv*	another	*no-r*
account	*accl.*	any	*ne*
addition	*adj*	application	*appl.*
additional	*adjl*	appreciate	*aprzl*
address	*adrs*	are	*r*
advertising	*advlr*	area	*rea*
advise	*advs*	as	*z*
after	*fr*	assistant	*assl.*
again	*agn*	association	*assn.*
against	*agns*	at	*@*
agent	*agl*	attached	*alc.*
ago	*ago*	attend	*ald*
all	*l*	attention	*alln.*
already	*lrd*	available	*avab*
also	*lso*	average	*avg*
always	*lwas*	back	*bk*
am	*am*	basis	*bss*
amount	*aml.*	be	*b*

NOTE: This dictionary contains the 422 most used words, according to Silverthorn's study (which is discussed in detail in the Appendix). When a root word is not among those 422 words and another form of the word is, the root word is not listed but the other form of the word is. For example "attach," "certain," and "deliver" are not listed but "attached," "certainly," and "delivery" are.

because	*bkz*	charge	*cg*
been	*bn*	check	*ck*
before	*bf*	city	*sl*
being	*b.*	claim	*klm*
believe	*blv*	class	*kls*
below	*blo*	college	*klg*
benefit	*bnfl*	come	*k*
best	*bS*	committee	*kml*
better	*blr*	company	*co.*
big	*bg*	complete	*kpll*
bill	*bl*	concerning	*ksrn.*
board	*bd*	continue	*conl*
bonds	*bds*	contract	*klrk*
book	*bk*	convenience	*kvnns*
both	*b—*	convention	*kvng*
box	*bx*	cooperation	*koprg*
bring	*br.*	copy	*kp*
building	*bldg.*	cordially	*c*
business	*bzns*	correct	*krk*
but	*bl*	cost	*kS*
by	*b*	could	*kd*
call	*kl*	county	*co.*
can	*kn*	course	*kre*
cannot	*kn*	cover	*kvr*
card	*kd*	credit	*kdl*
care	*kr*	current	*krl*
cash	*kz*	customer	*kSmr*
certainly	*slnl*	date	*dl*
certificate	*slfkl*	day	*da*
chairman	*crm*	dealer	*dlr*
change	*cg*	dear	*d*

defense	*dfns*	farm	*fm*
delivery	*dlvr*	federal	*fdrl*
department	*dpt*	feel	*fl*
desire	*dzr*	few	*fu*
did	*dd*	field	*fld*
direct	*drk*	fill	*f*
director	*dir.*	find	*fd*
district	*dstk*	first	*fs*
division	*div.*	following	*flo.*
do	*du*	for	*4*
does	*ds*	form	*fm*
done	*dn*	forward	*fwd*
don't	*dl*	found	*fwd*
due	*du*	four	*4*
during	*dr.*	free	*fr*
each	*ea.*	friend	*frd*
education	*educ*	from	*fm*
effective	*fkv*	full	*f*
either	*e-r*	furnish	*fnz*
employees	*mple*	further	*f-r*
enclosed	*enc.*	future	*fulr*
enclosing	*enc.*	general	*gen*
enclosure	*encl.*	gentlemen	*g*
equipment	*eqp*	get	*gt*
even	*evn*	give	*gv*
ever	*evr*	glad	*gld*
every	*evr*	go	*go*
experience	*yprns*	good	*gd*
extra	*ytra*	government	*gvt.*
fact	*fk*	great	*grt*
family	*fml*	group	*gp*

Word	Shorthand	Word	Shorthand
had	*hd*	invoice	*nvos*
hand	*hd*	is	*z*
happy	*hp*	issue	*izu*
has	*h*	it	*t*
have	*hv*	items	*tms*
he	*he*	its	*ts*
head	*hd*	job	*jb*
hear	*hr*	just	*js*
held	*hld*	keep	*kp*
help	*hlp*	kind	*kd*
here	*hr*	know	*no*
high	*hi*	large	*lrg*
him	*hm*	last	*ls*
his	*hs*	less	*ls*
home	*hm*	let	*ll*
hope	*hp*	letter	*llr*
hospital	*hosp.*	life	*lf*
how	*hw*	like	*lk*
however	*hwvr*	line	*ln*
I	*i*	list	*ls*
if	*f*	little	*lll*
immediately	*mdll*	loan	*ln*
important	*mpl*	long	*lng*
in	*n*	look	*lk*
income	*nk*	low	*lo*
increase	*incr.*	made	*md*
information	*nfo.*	mail	*ml*
insurance	*ins.*	make	*mk*
interest	*ns*	manager	*mgr.*
into	*no*	many	*me*
investment	*nvsm*	market	*mkl*

material	*mtrl*	office	*ofs*
may	*ma*	old	*ol*
me	*me*	on	*n*
meeting	*mt.*	one	*1*
member	*mbr*	only	*onl*
membership	*mbrzp*	operation	*opry*
men	*m*	opportunity	*optnt*
merchandise	*mrcdns*	or	*r*
might	*mt*	order	*rdr*
miss	*m*	organization	*org.*
money	*me*	other	*otr*
month	*mo.*	our	*r*
more	*mr*	out	*ut*
most	*ms*	over	*o*
much	*mc*	own	*on*
my	*my*	page	*pg*
name	*nm*	paid	*pd*
national	*ntl.*	part	*pt*
necessary	*ncsr*	past	*ps*
need	*nd*	pay	*pa*
never	*nvr*	payment	*pam*
new	*nu*	people	*ppl*
next	*nx*	per	*p*
no	*no*	period	*pd*
not	*n*	personal	*psnl*
note	*nt*	persons	*psnz*
notice	*nts*	place	*pls*
now	*nw*	plan	*pln*
number	*no.*	please	*plz*
of	*v*	pleasure	*plzr*
offer	*of*	policy	*plc*

position	*pos.*	remain	*rmn*
possible	*psb*	remember	*rmbr*
post	*ps*	reply	*rple*
power	*pwr*	report	*rpt*
premium	*pmm*	representative	*rp*
present	*psl*	request	*rks*
president	*pres.*	required	*rkr*
price	*pr.*	requirements	*rkrmz*
probably	*pbbl*	reserve	*rsv*
problems	*pblmz*	return	*rtn*
product	*pdk*	right	*rt*
program	*pgrm*	room	*rm*
protection	*ptkj*	sale	*sl*
provide	*pvd*	same	*sm*
public	*pblc*	sample	*smpl*
purchase	*pcs*	savings	*sv.z*
put	*pt*	say	*sa*
quality	*kwll*	school	*skl*
question	*?*	secretary	*sec*
rate	*rt*	section	*sec.*
read	*rd*	sell	*sl*
real	*rl*	send	*sd*
reason	*rzn*	sent	*st*
receipt	*rsp*	serve	*sv*
receive	*rsv*	service	*svs*
recent	*rsl*	set	*st*
record	*rkd*	several	*svrl*
reference	*rf.*	shall	*gl*
regarding	*rgd.*	sheet	*zt*
regular	*rg*	shipment	*zpm*
regulations	*rgs*	should	*zd*

show	*zo*	their	*—r,*
since	*sns*	them	*—m*
sincerely	*s*	then	*—n*
sir	*s*	there	*—r,*
size	*sz*	therefore	*—rf*
small	*sml*	these	*—z*
so	*so*	they	*—a*
sold	*sld*	think	*—k*
some	*sm*	this	*s*
soon	*sn*	those	*—oz*
special	*spy*	three	*3*
state	*St*	through	*—ru*
statement	*Stm*	time	*tm*
still	*Sl*	to	*2*
stock	*Sk*	total	*ttl*
store	*Sr,*	trade	*trd*
students	*Stls*	training	*trn.*
study	*Sd*	truly	*l*
subject	*sjk*	two	*2*
such	*sc*	type	*tp*
suggest	*sgs*	under	*u*
supply	*spl*	unless	*nls*
sure	*zr*	until	*ntl*
system	*stm*	up	*up*
take	*tk*	upon	*upn*
tax	*tx*	us	*s*
tell	*tl*	use	*uz*
than	*—n*	value	*vlu*
thank	*—k*	various	*vrs*
that	*l*	very	*v*
the	*—*	want	*wt*

war	*wr*
was	*wz*
way	*wa*
we	*w*
week	*wk*
well	*l*
were	*wr*
what	*wl*
when	*wn*
where	*wr*
which	*wc*
while	*wl*
who	*ho*
why	*y*
will	*l*
wish	*wz*
with	*w*
within	*wn*
without	*wwl*
work	*wk*
world	*wrld*
would	*wd*
write	*rl*
year	*yr*
yet	*yl*
you	*u*
your	*u*
yours	*u*

Index